How to Draw Cartoon Farm Animals (This Book on How to Draw Farm Animals Will Show You How to Draw 40 Farm Animals Step by Step)

This how to draw farm animals book contains lots of advice on how to draw 40 different farm animals easily

James Manning

How to Draw Cartoon Farm Animals

Introduction for Parents

Drawing is an essential part of a child's development, stimulating parts of the brain that are responsible for creative thinking and imagination. From a young age, we are all creatively encouraged to draw, whether it be at home or pre-school. Drawing is often encouraged to improve our fine motor skills and hand-eye co-ordination; this co-ordination is vital for future academic success and for improving our penmanship/handwriting skills.

From toddler's 'scribbles' to more refined 'matchstick men' and recognisable shapes, you may find that as your child grows they will want to tackle a more complex way of drawing (perhaps it's an image they have seen in a book) but as they begin to put pencil to paper they may have no idea where to start, causing frustration and annoyance.

With the help of our 'How to Draw' book series, this frustration will disappear as we guide your child step by step, line by line, to create their very own masterpiece!

Each illustration is deconstructed and simplified into lines and shapes which will not overwhelm your child. As we guide them to form each simple line and shape together on the paper, the image gradually becomes more detailed, textured and visually appealing. Practice will always make perfect, so encouraging your child to repeat the initial steps will incite a sense of self assurance that they are able to improve their skill line by line.

If Your Child Struggles With This Book

The rate of cognitive development varies from child to child and, as such, where one child may be ready for this book another will not. If you feel that your child is not ready for this book at the moment, take it away and bring it back to them in six to twelve months.

If your child is not ready to draw step-by-step, he or she may prefer to work using grids. Grid drawing involves copying information from one grid to another using coordinates. The type of copying required in grid drawing is very useful for the brain as, in particular, it exercises working memory. Working memory involves holding onto information temporarily and then using that temporarily held information at the same time. Working memory is an important process required in maintaining attention and exercising it will be beneficial for a range of activities, including in class at school.

Dr James Manning
Consultant Clinical Psychologist

For the webpage and password for your bonus books please see bottom of page 40.

HOW TO DRAW CARTOON FARM ANIMALS

Here are all of the drawings in this book. I guess it must seem like there is a lot of them when they are looked at all at once!

Luckily, I am not going to ask you to draw them all straight away. The best way to learn to draw is one step at a time. Each drawing in this book may require between 50 and 200 strokes of your pencil, but all you will need to think about is drawing one stroke at a time.

As you use your pencil, stroke by stroke, working your way through this book, you will eventually be able to create all of the drawings!

Drawing Step-by-Step

In this book I will show you how to create 40 different drawings step by step. Each step will build on the previous one until eventually you have 40 complete drawings.

To make things easier for you, please download the outline grids for the drawings. You can download this additional book with all of them inside for free by visiting the web address below:

https://www.lipdf.com/product/farmanimals/

At first, you find my step-by-step approach too complicated or difficult please leave it to one side and come back to it later. Instead, you may want to use an alternative grid with numbers and letters on it first. By following the coordinates and matching them up with the coordinates on a blank grid you can redraw the pictures this way instead.

I have put details below about where you can download these basic grids for free on the internet.

https://www.lipdf.com/product/grids/

You can of course ask an adult to help you draw the grids instead, or you may even feel able to draw them yourself.

Please see page 40 for the webpage address for your bonus books and the password.

1. Although this is the first character in the book, you don't have to start drawing here! Flick through the book and find your favourite drawing to start with.

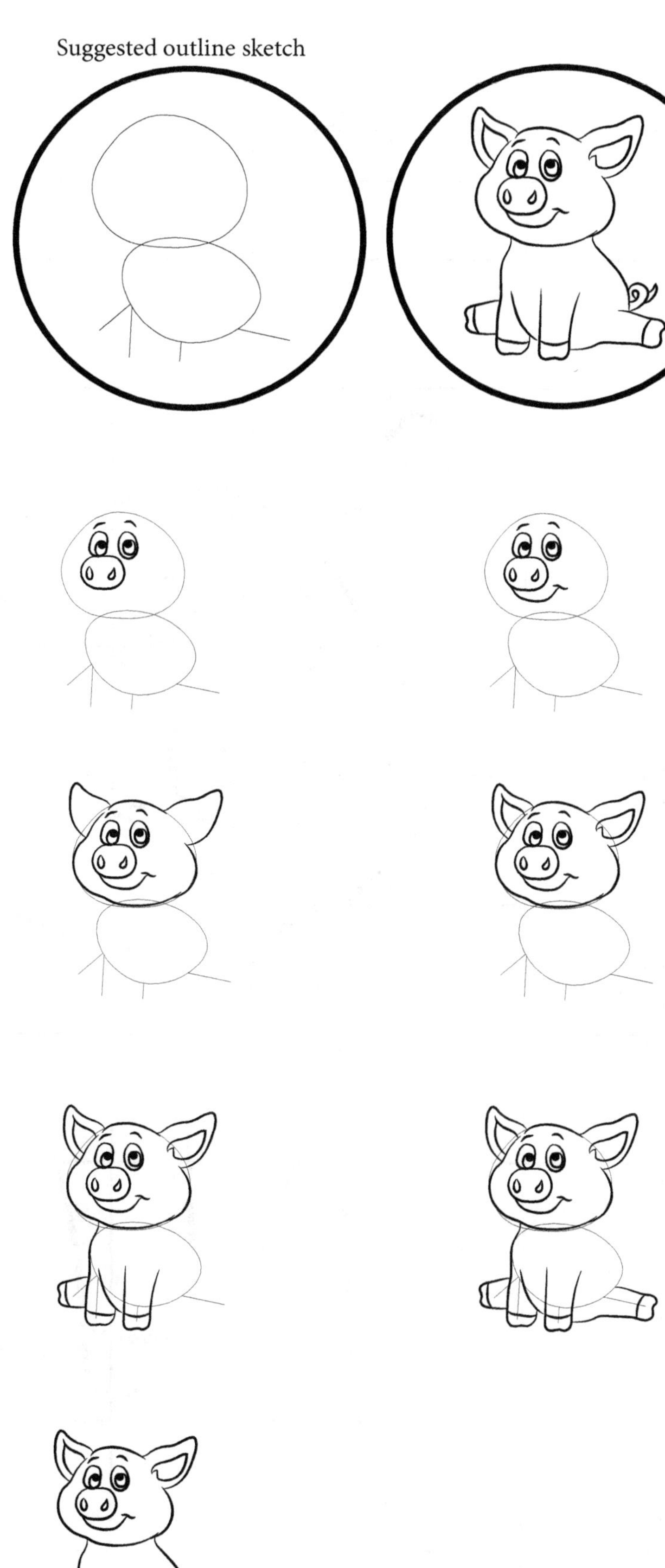

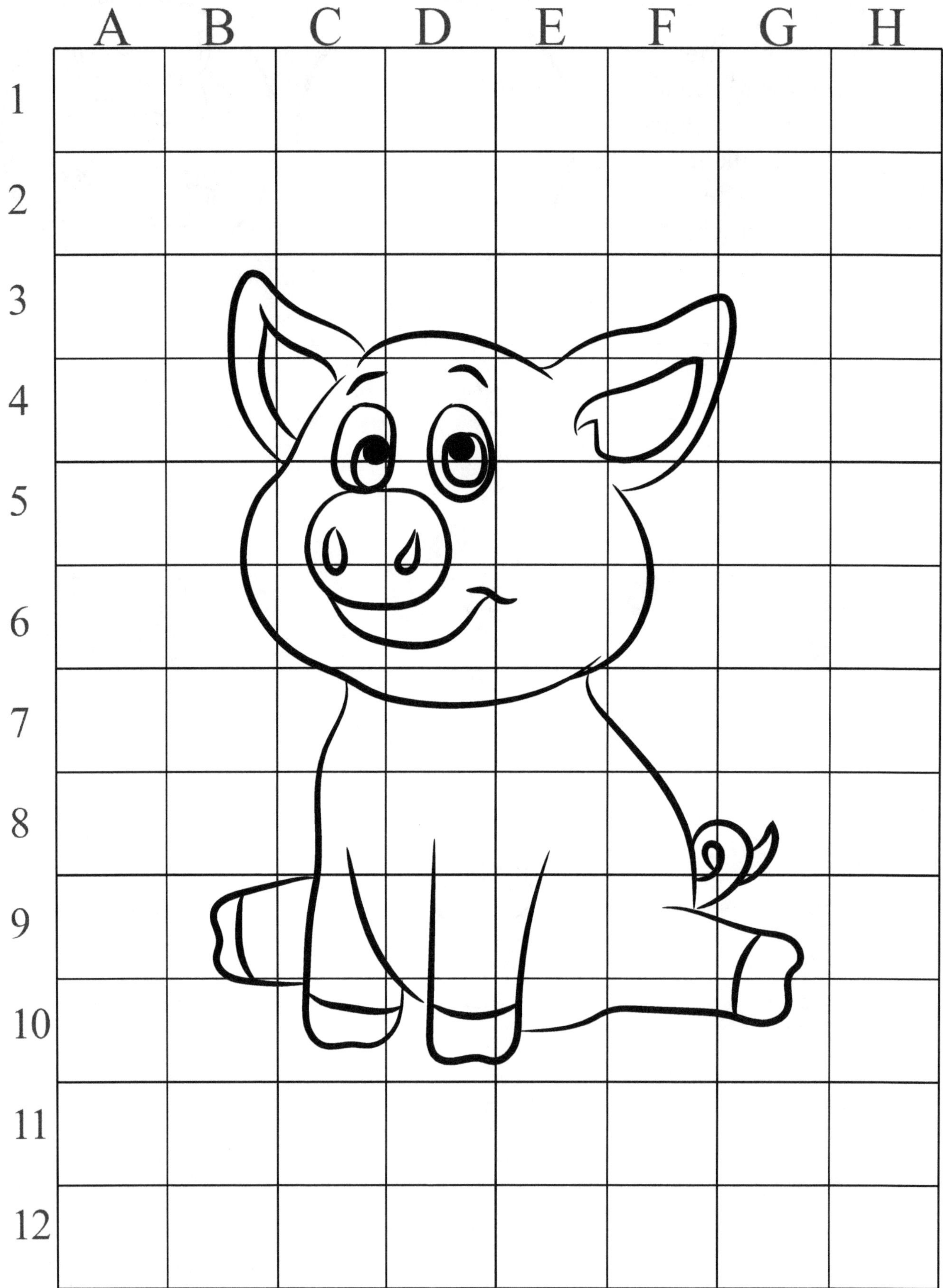

A B C D E F G H
1
2
3
4
5
6
7
8
9
10
11
12

2. Keep practicing. It's often helpful if you use a pencil so you can erase anything you think is a mistake.

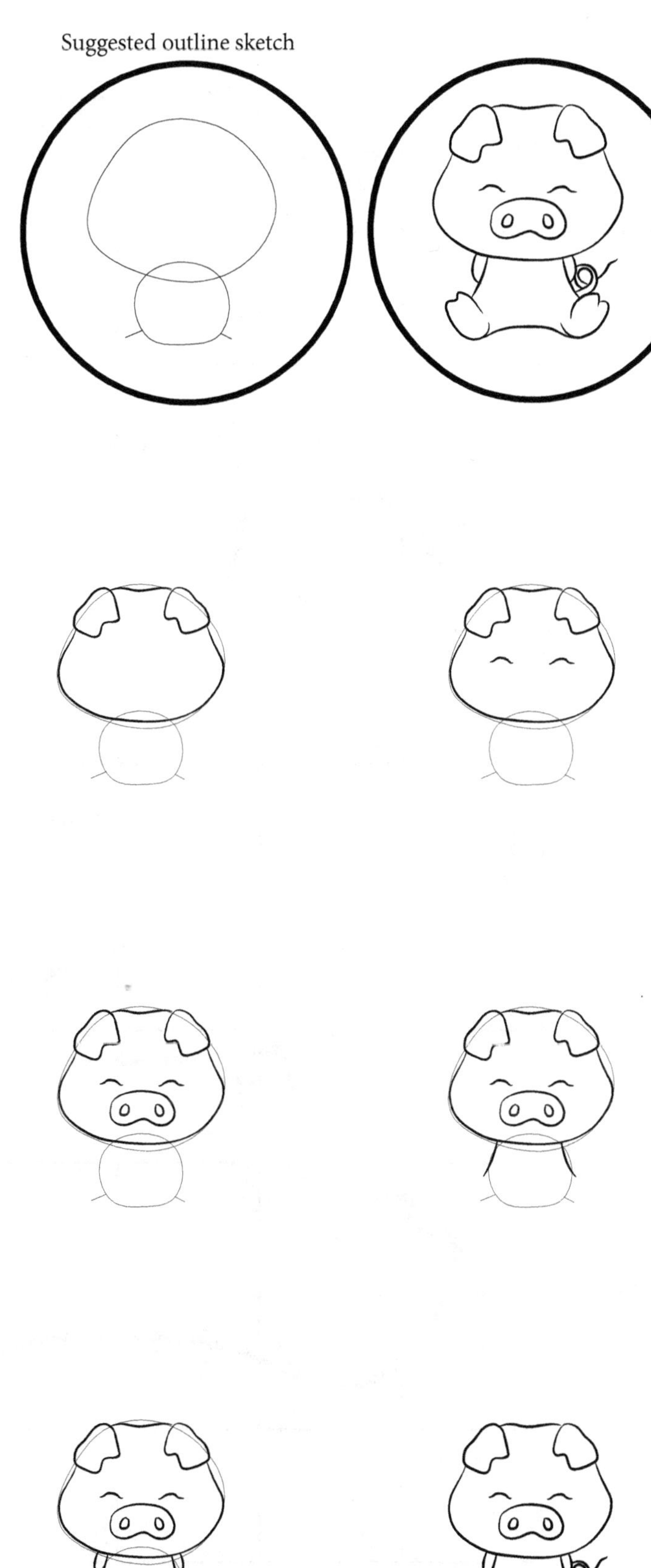

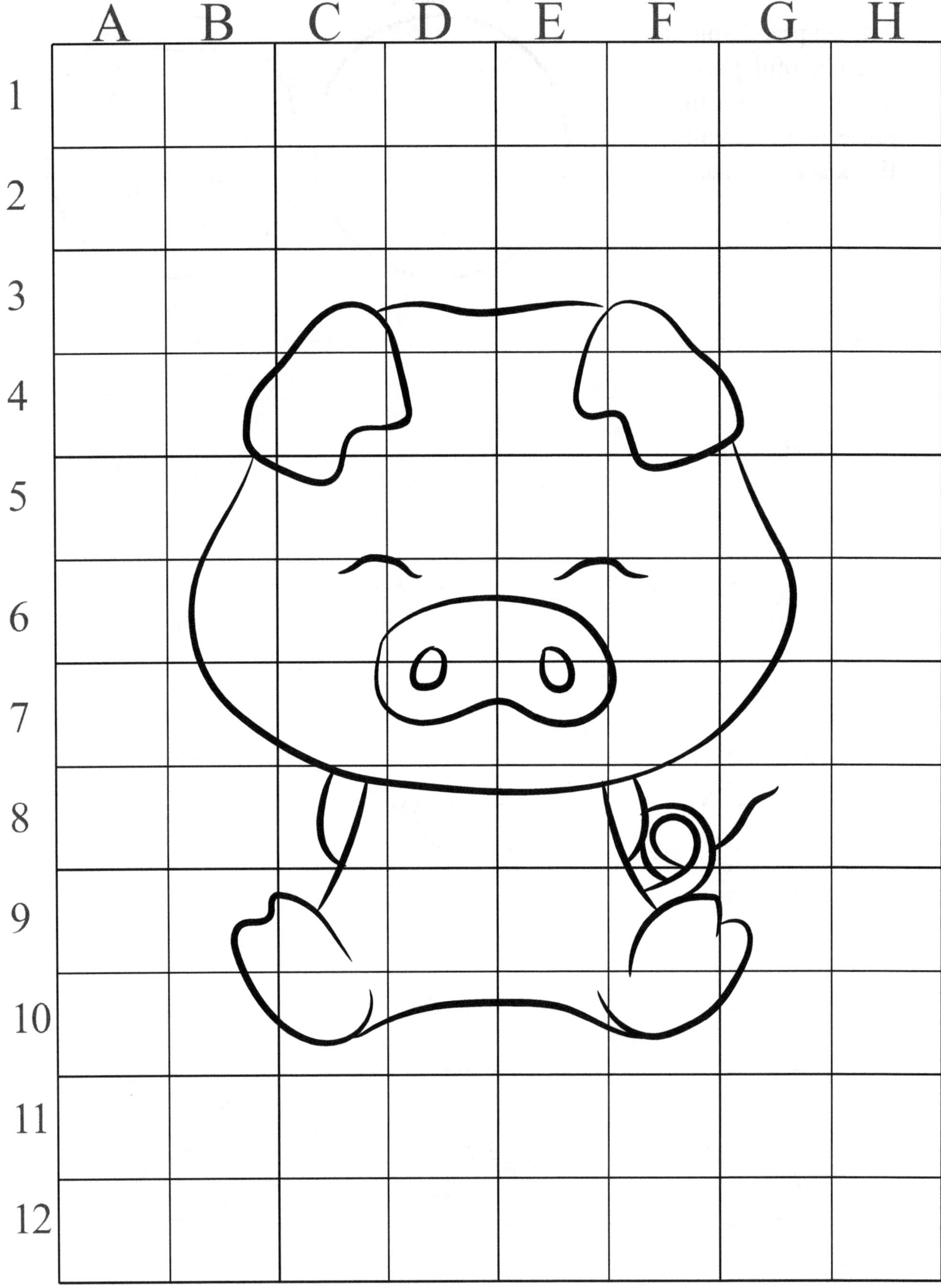

A B C D E F G H
1
2
3
4
5
6
7
8
9
10
11
12

3. The first stroke of your pencil can often be the most daunting but give it a go and see where the drawing takes you!

Suggested outline sketch

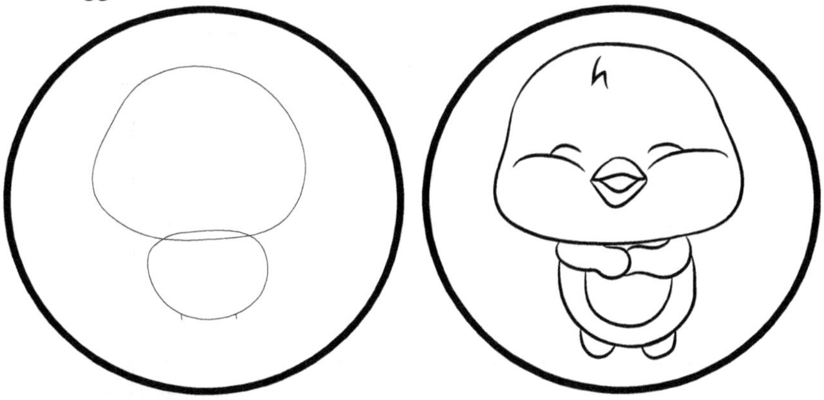

A B C D E F G H

Suggested outline sketch

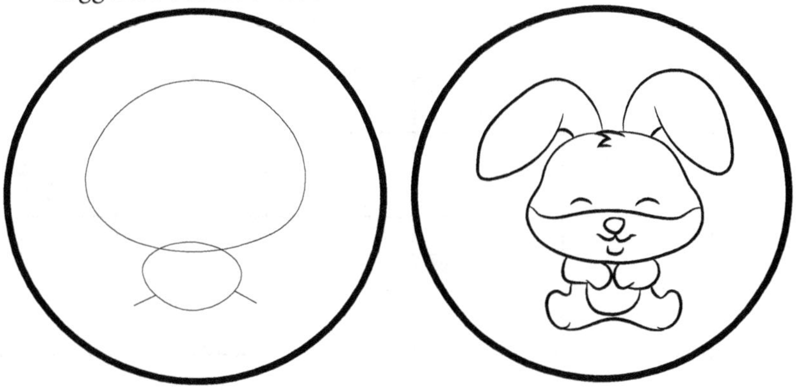

4. The mouth on this particular character is a single pencil stroke, how about changing the direction of the stroke to change how the character is feeling? Are they happy, sad, upset…etc?

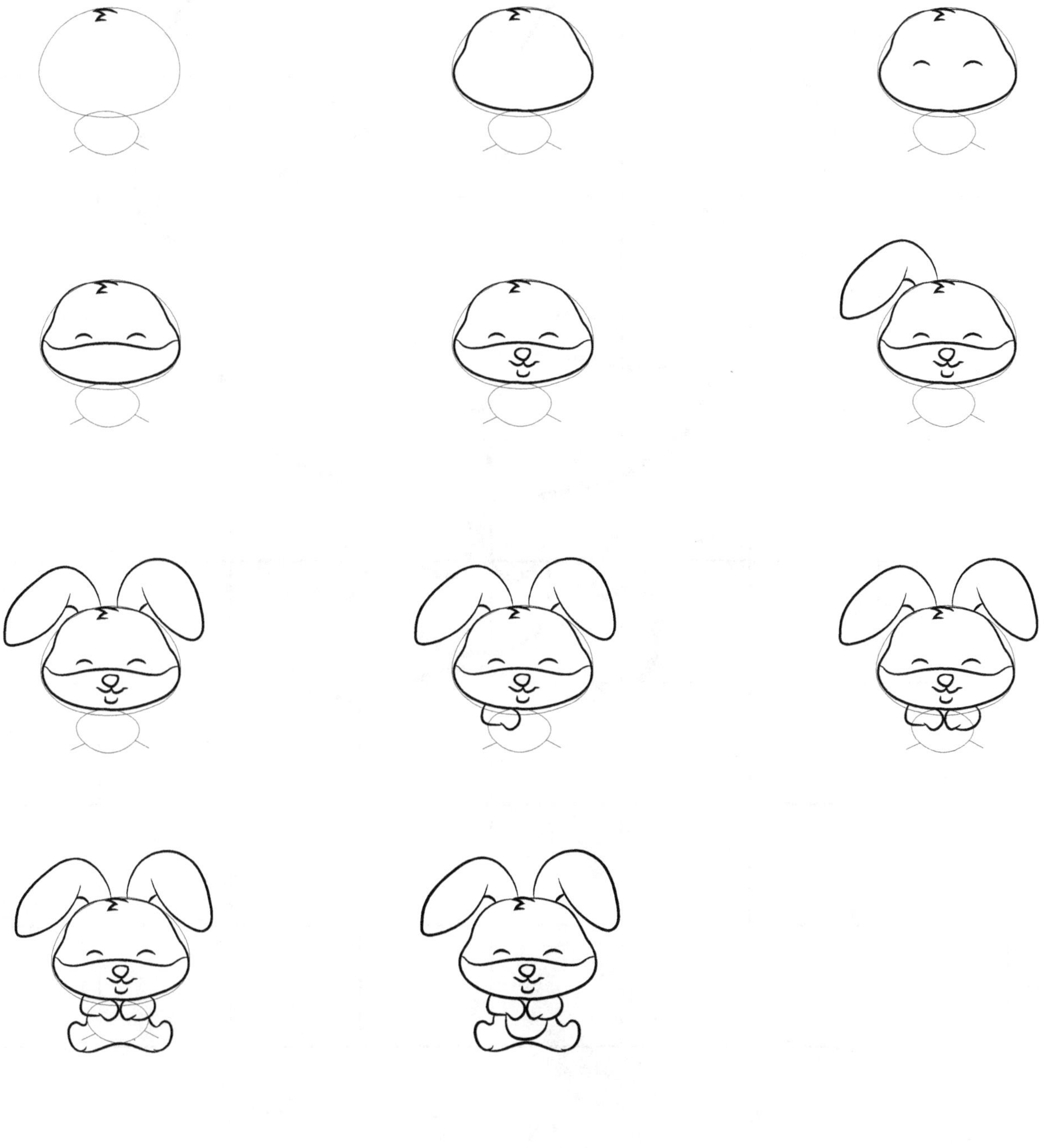

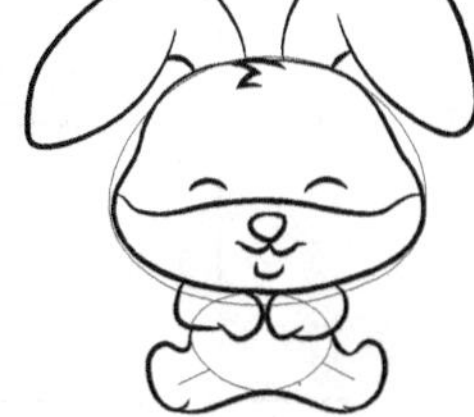

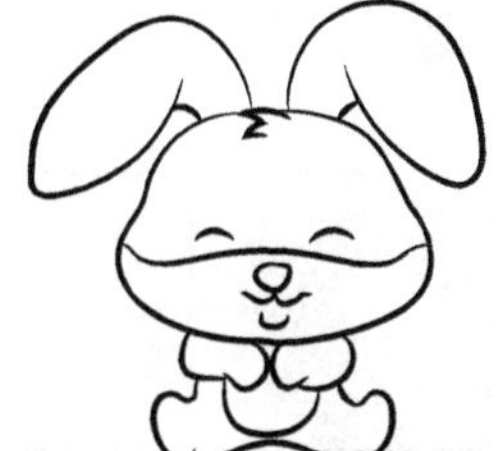

A B C D E F G H
1
2
3
4
5
6
7
8
9
10
11
12

5. Copying the lines exactly as they are shown in the book isn't a necessity, use the grids as a guide and source of inspiration for your own drawing.

Suggested outline sketch

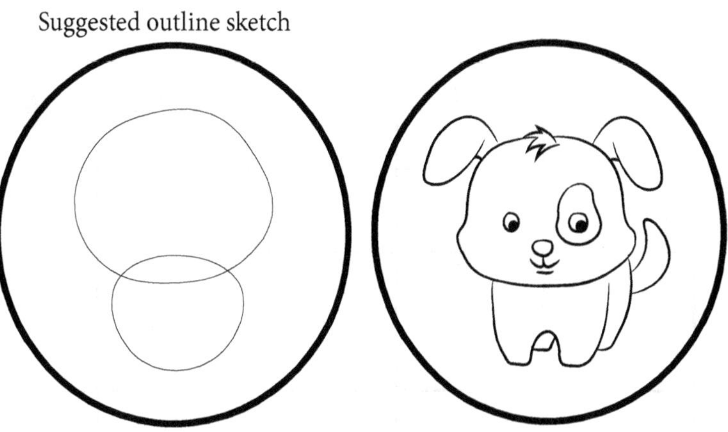

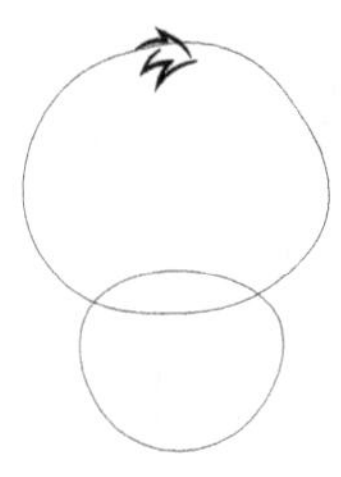

A B C D E F G H
1 2 3 4 5 6 7 8 9 10 11 12

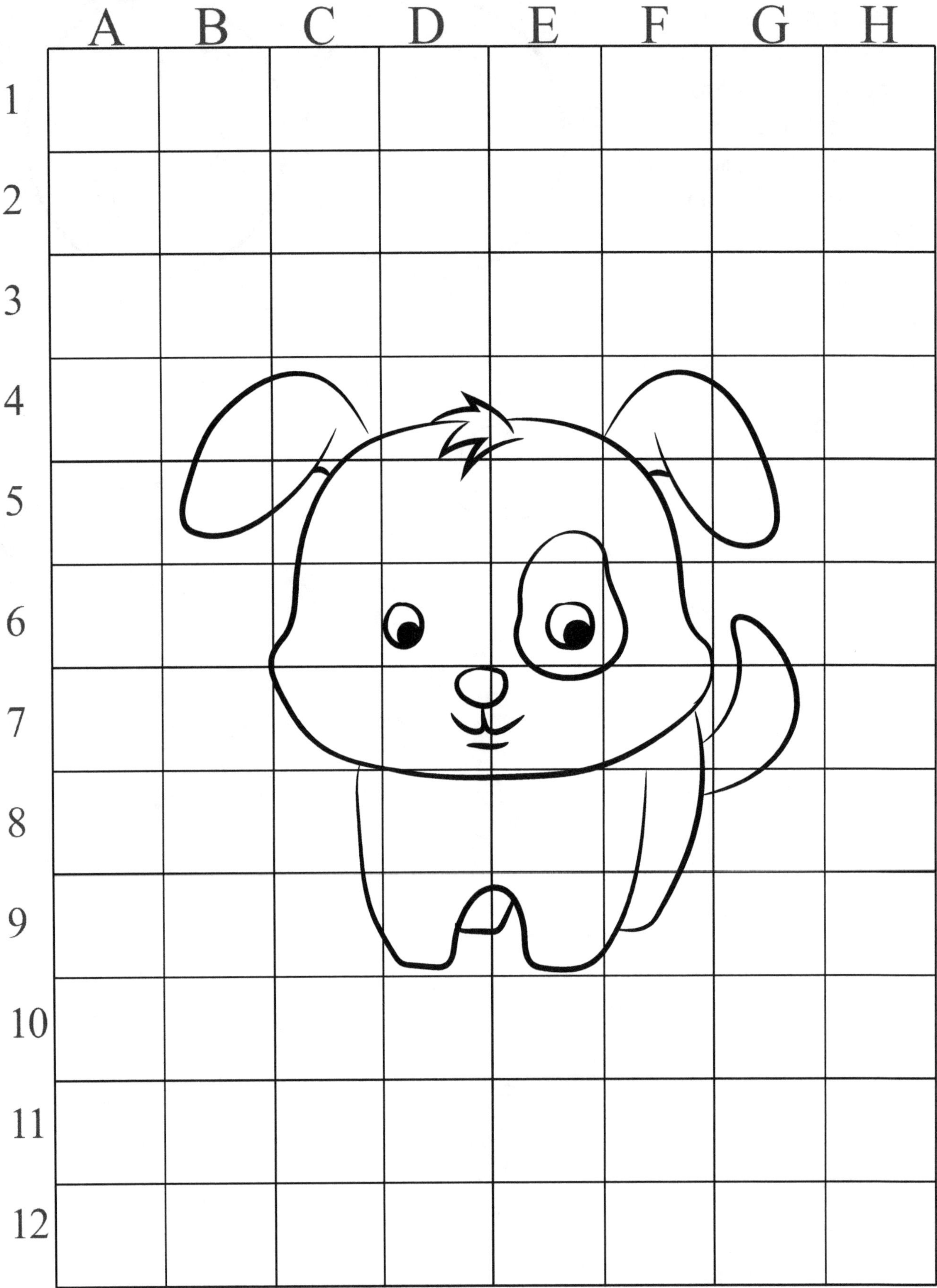

6. Don't get frustrated if you can't copy the lines exactly, just use them to point you in the right direction.

Suggested outline sketch

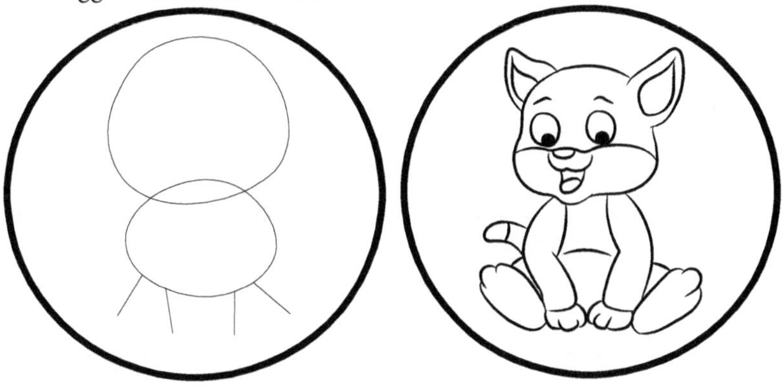

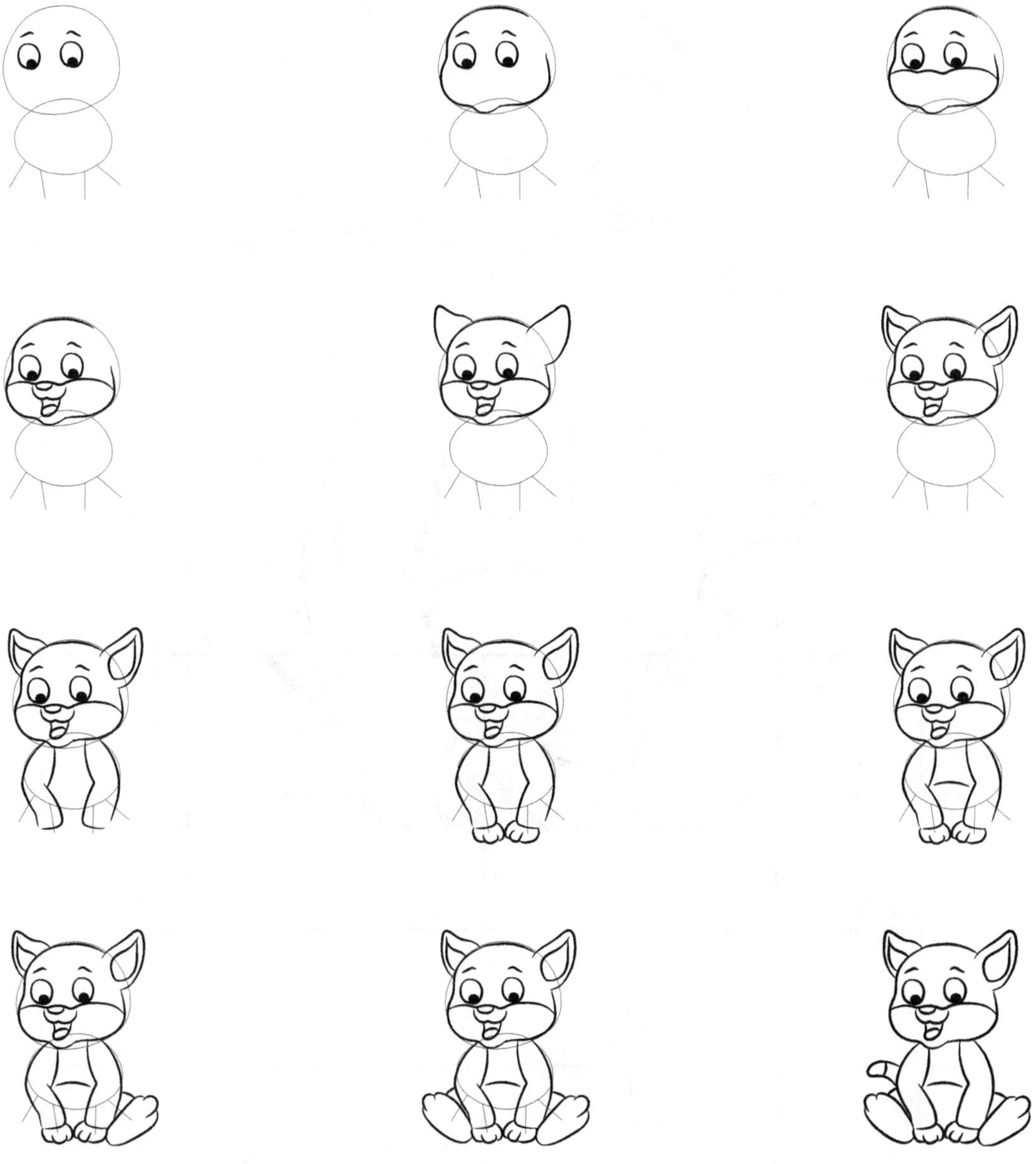

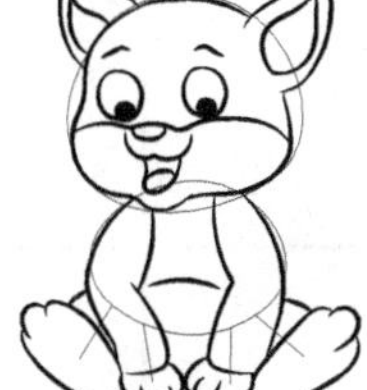

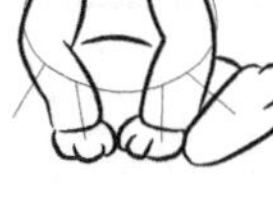

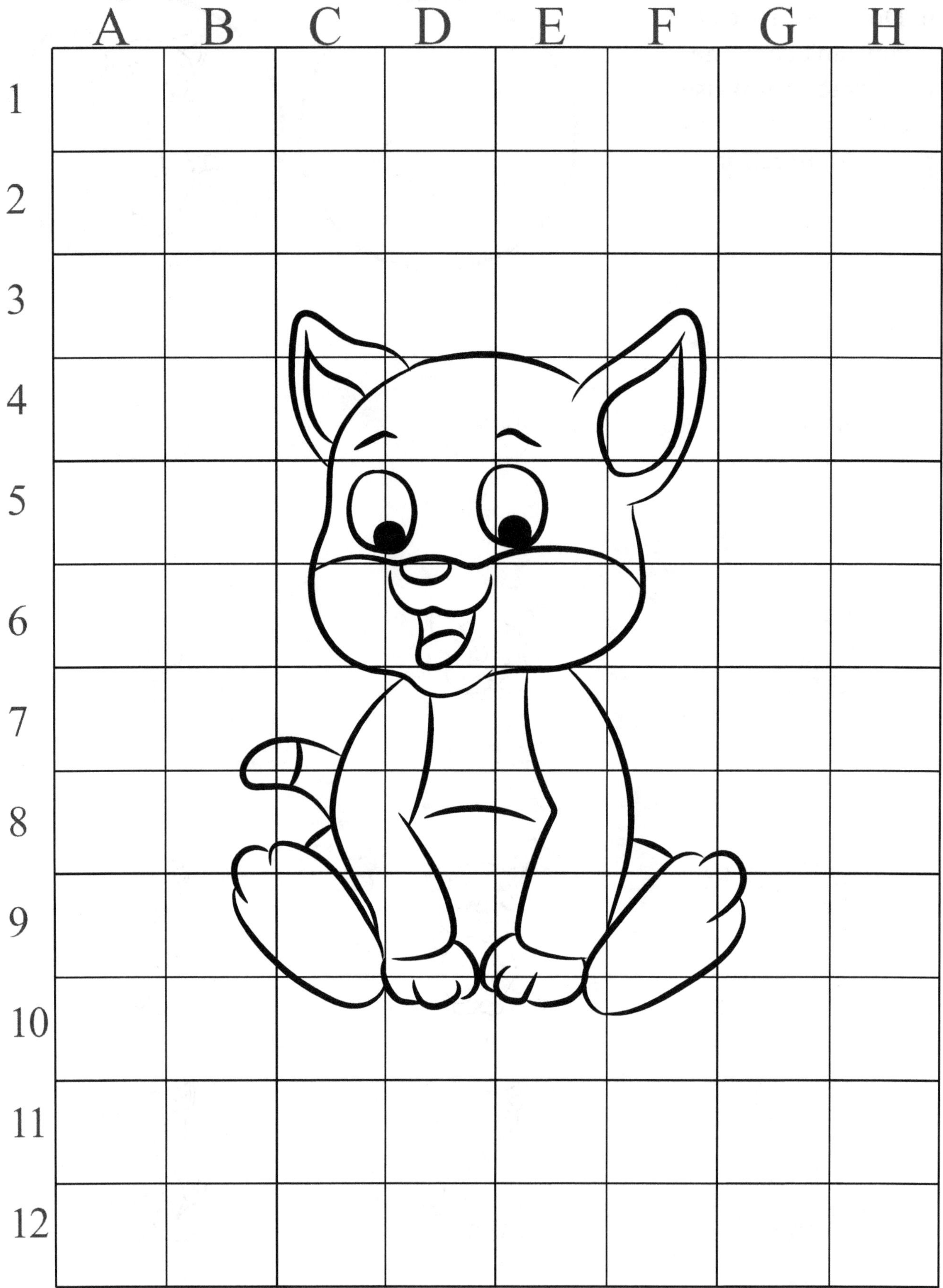

A B C D E F G H
1
2
3
4
5
6
7
8
9
10
11
12

7. If you find you are getting frustrated with your drawing, take a break and come back to it later.

Suggested outline sketch

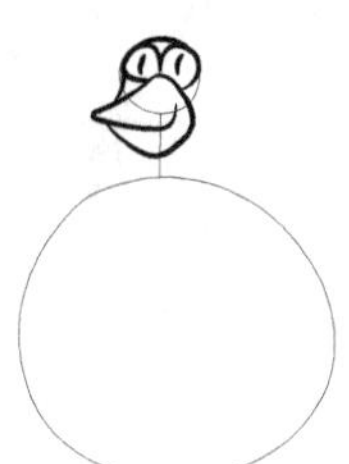

A B C D E F G H
1
2
3
4
5
6
7
8
9
10
11
12

8. Take your time and keep practicing, everybody learns at different paces.

A B C D E F G H
1
2
3
4
5
6
7
8
9
10
11
12

9. Don't worry if you are spending more time drawing a picture, it's more important to take your time when producing high quality work.

Suggested outline sketch

Try not to worry about how your character looks at this stage, once you have drawn in the other parts it will bring them to life!

A B C D E F G H
1
2
3
4
5
6
7
8
9
10
11
12

10. Don't forget the outline sketch is there to help you. Use it to help keep your drawing in proportion.

Suggested outline sketch

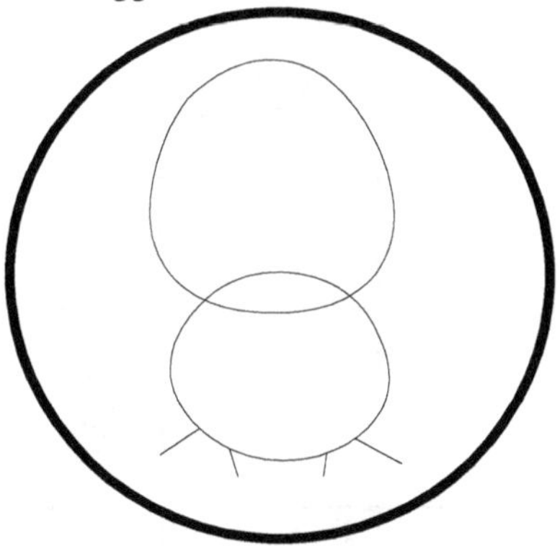

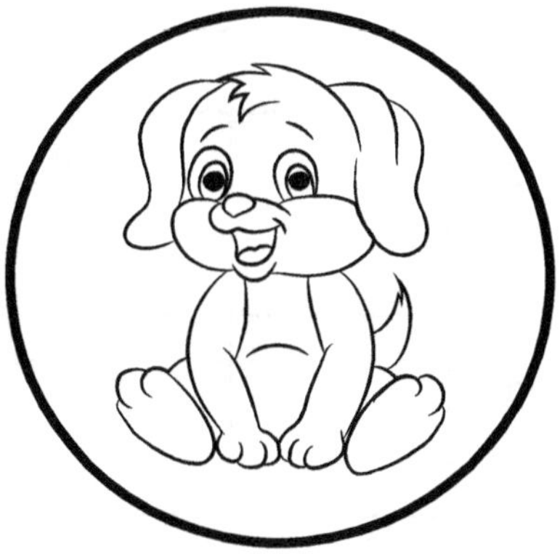

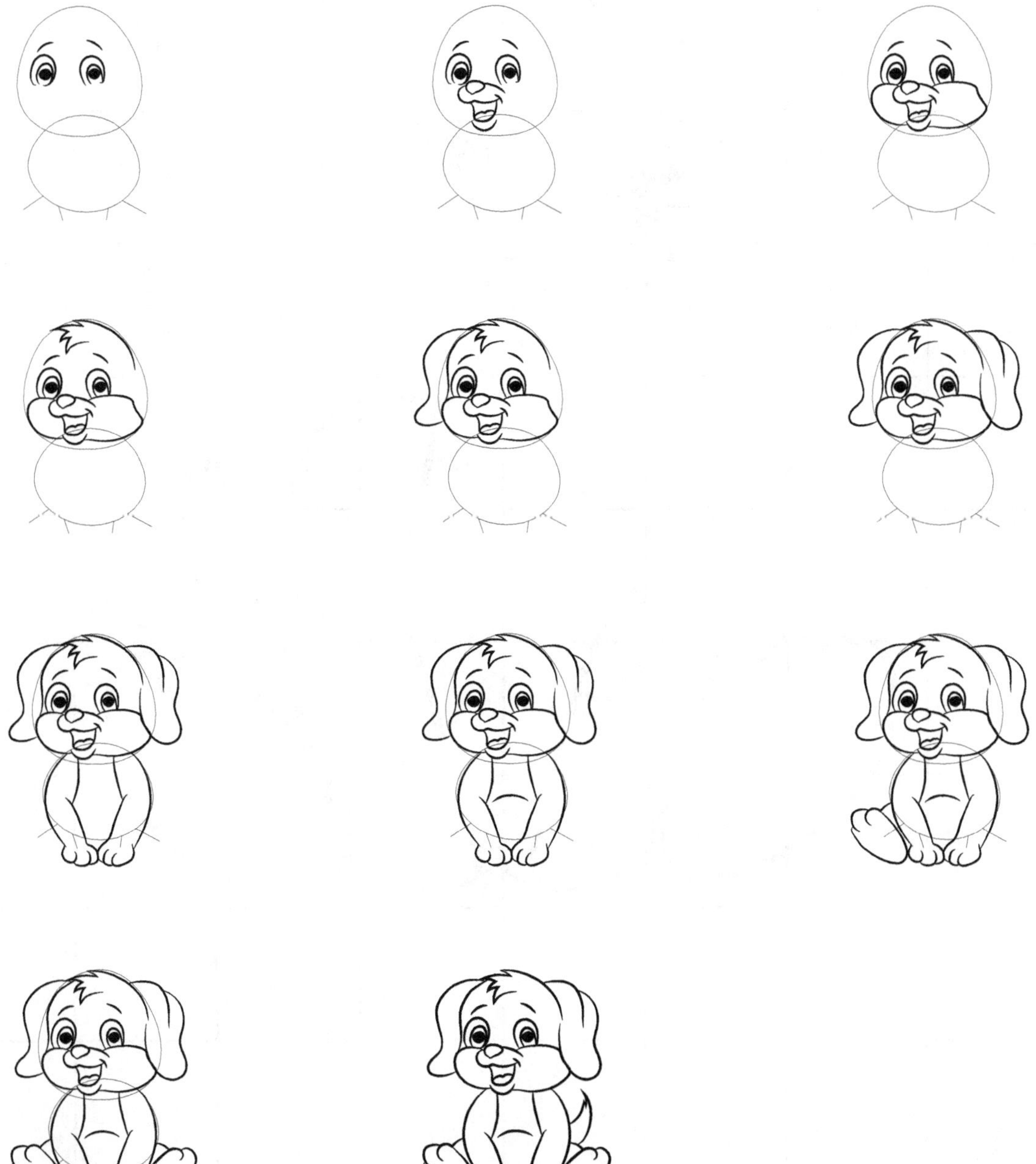

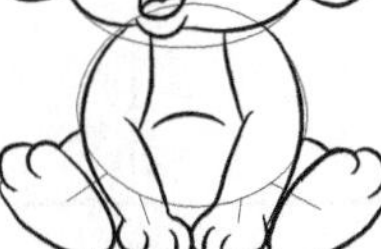

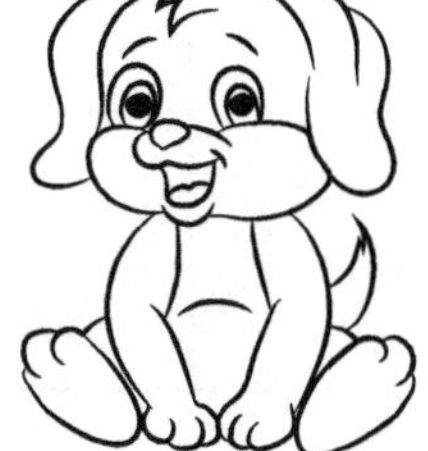

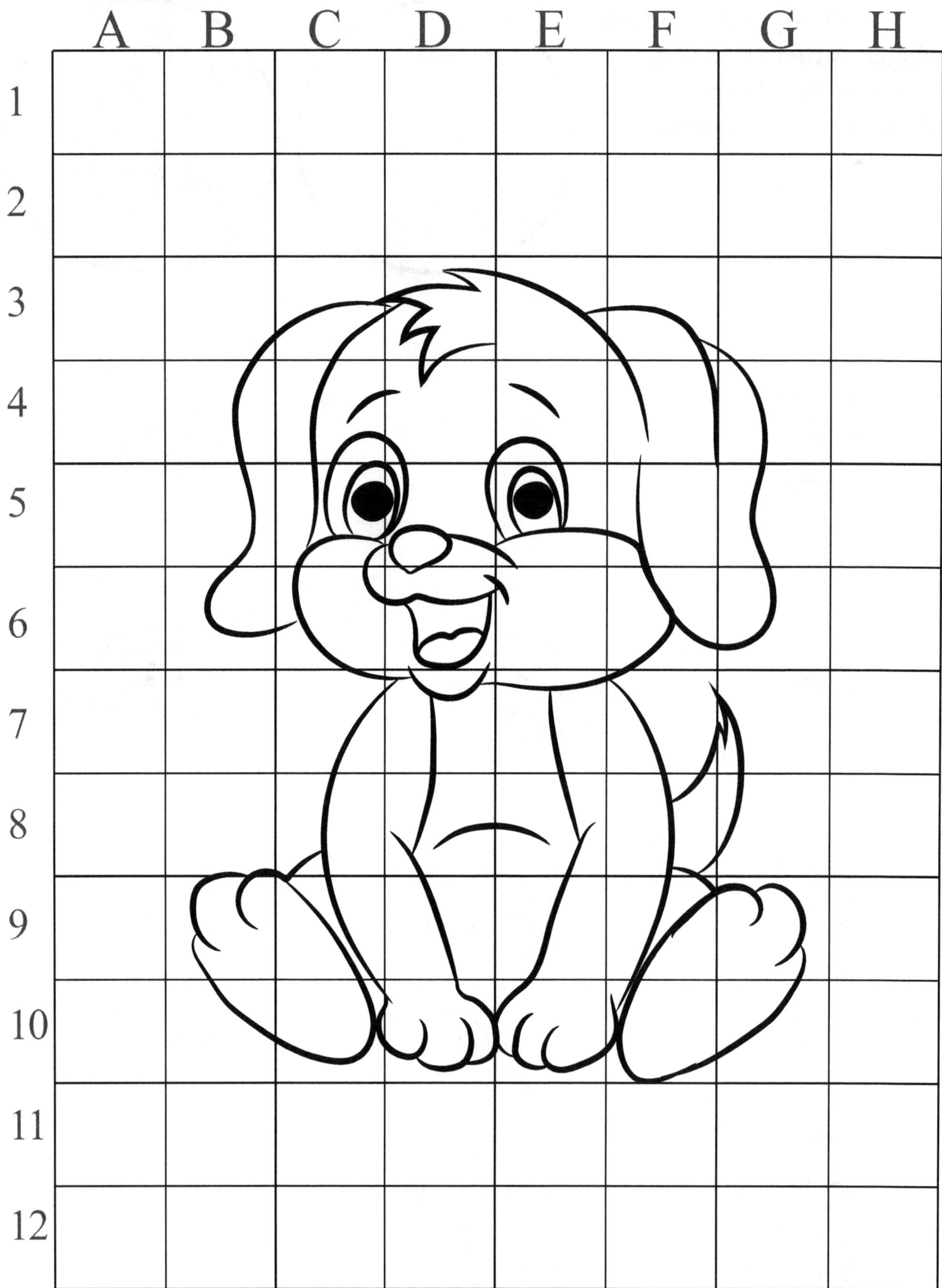

A B C D E F G H
1
2
3
4
5
6
7
8
9
10
11
12

11. A simple change such as moving the characters pupils in their eyes can make them seem like they are looking at something.

12. Add some colour
to the finished
drawing to really give
it some personality.

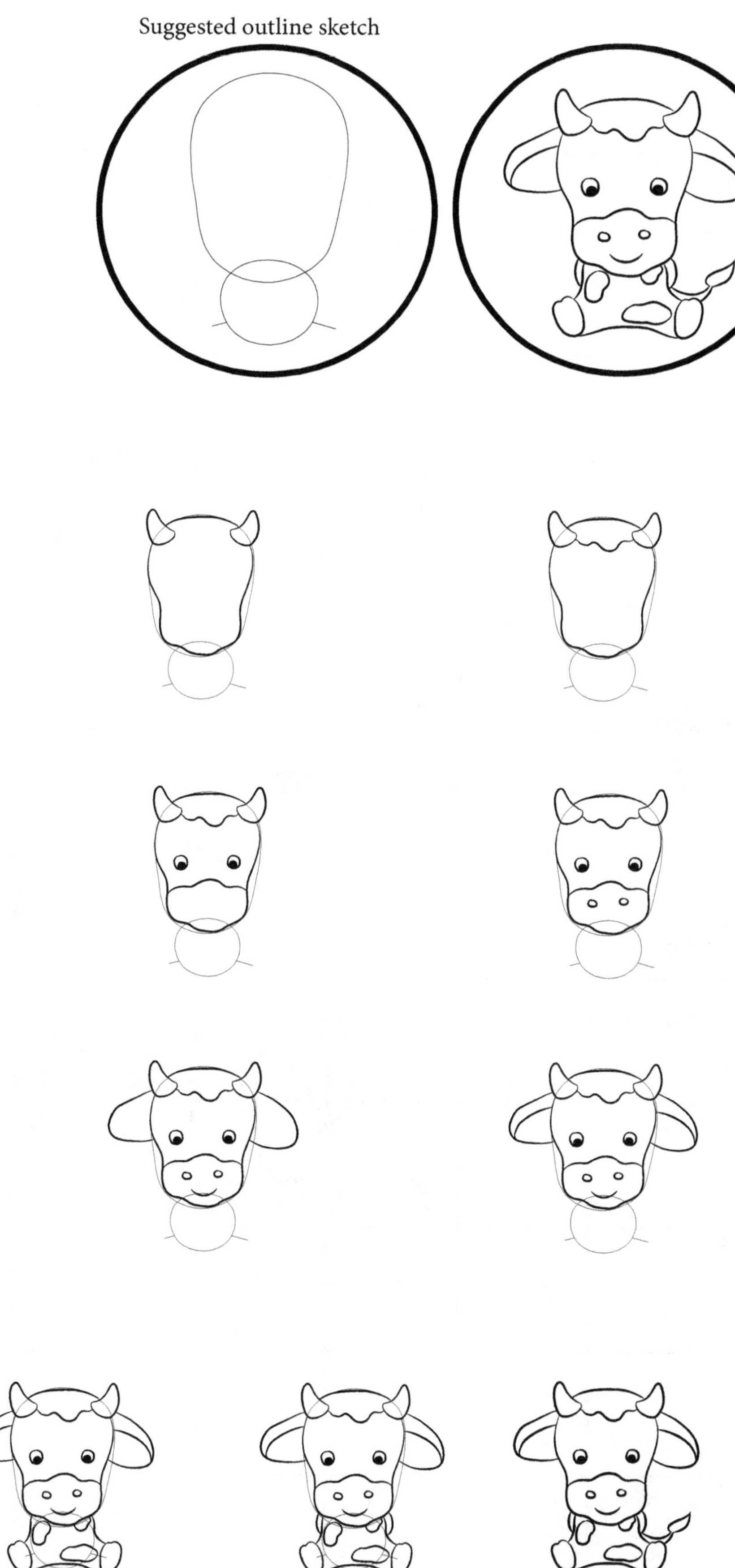

Suggested outline sketch

13. If you're using the
grid, take the drawing
one box at a time.

Suggested outline sketch

14. If you find you are
drawing the head too small
and are struggling to draw
in all the features, try
starting your drawing with
the eyes and mouth, then
draw in the shape of the
head afterwards.

Suggested outline sketch

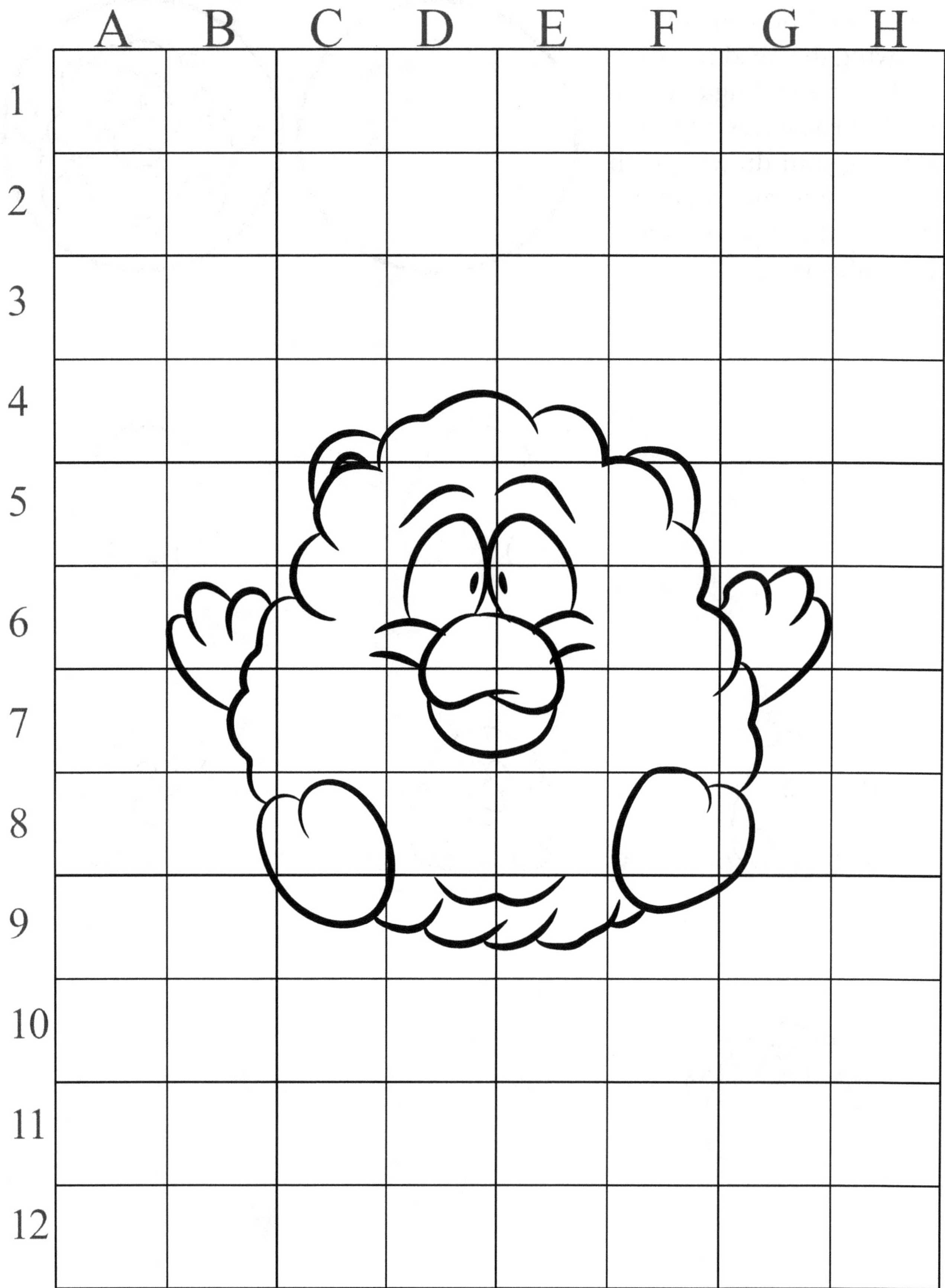

A B C D E F G H
1
2
3
4
5
6
7
8
9
10
11
12

15. Add in extra
features to make you
drawing unique and
personal to you.

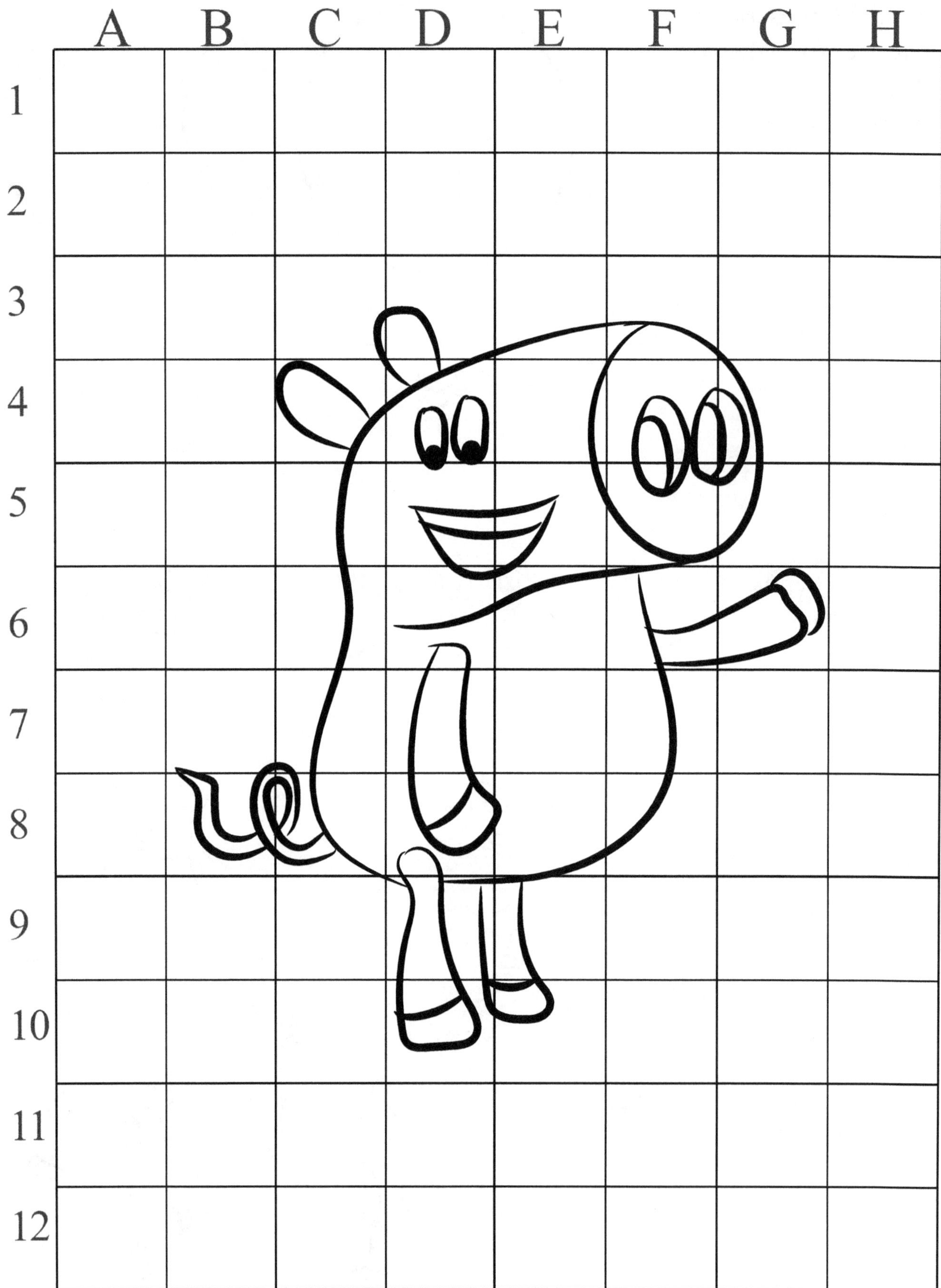

A B C D E F G H
1
2
3
4
5
6
7
8
9
10
11
12

16. Once you have practiced using grids, in the future you may be able to create your drawing from memory alone.

Suggested outline sketch

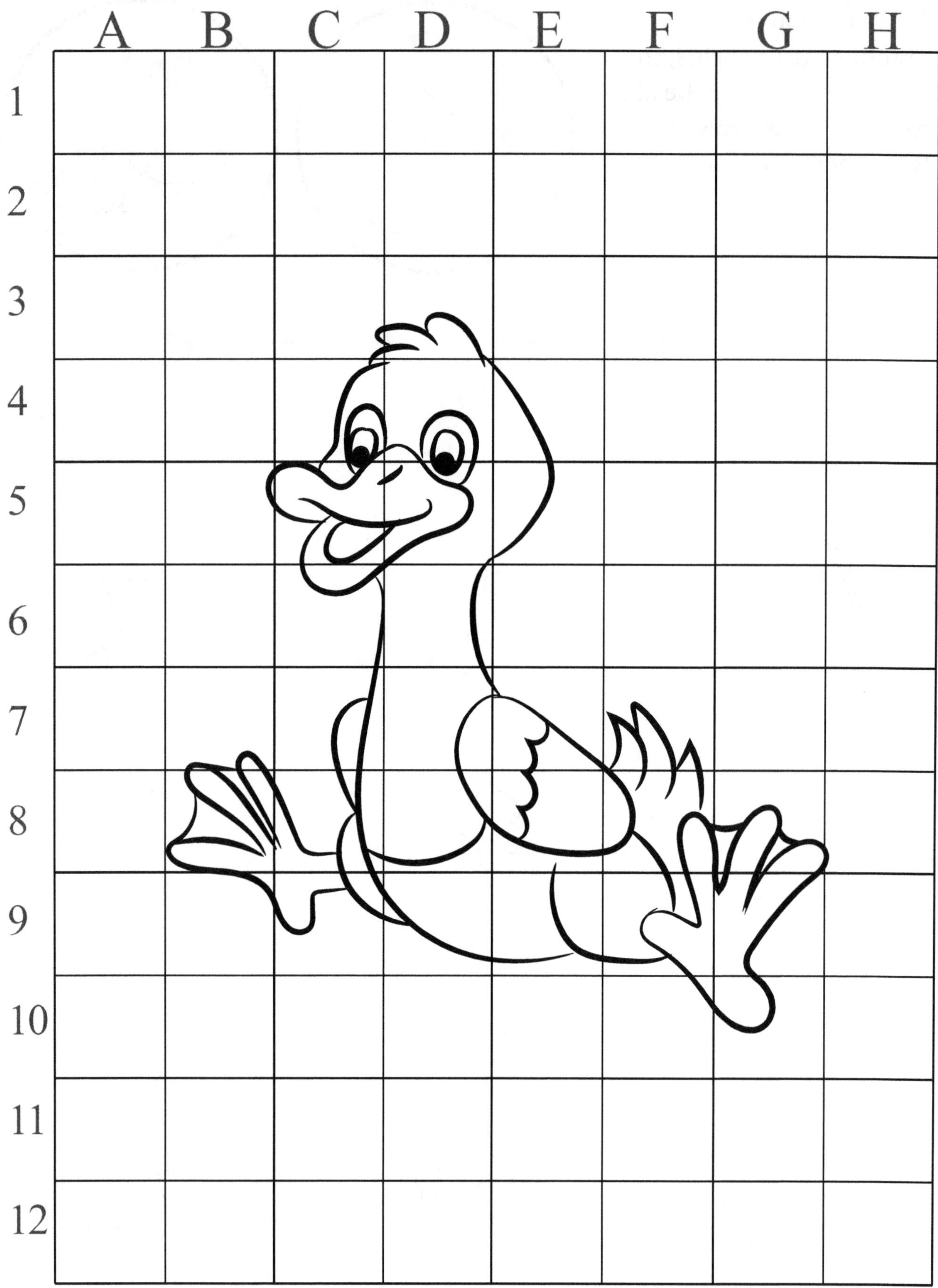

A B C D E F G H
1
2
3
4
5
6
7
8
9
10
11
12

17. It's unlikely you will get everything right the first time. Draw in pencil so you can erase any mistakes.

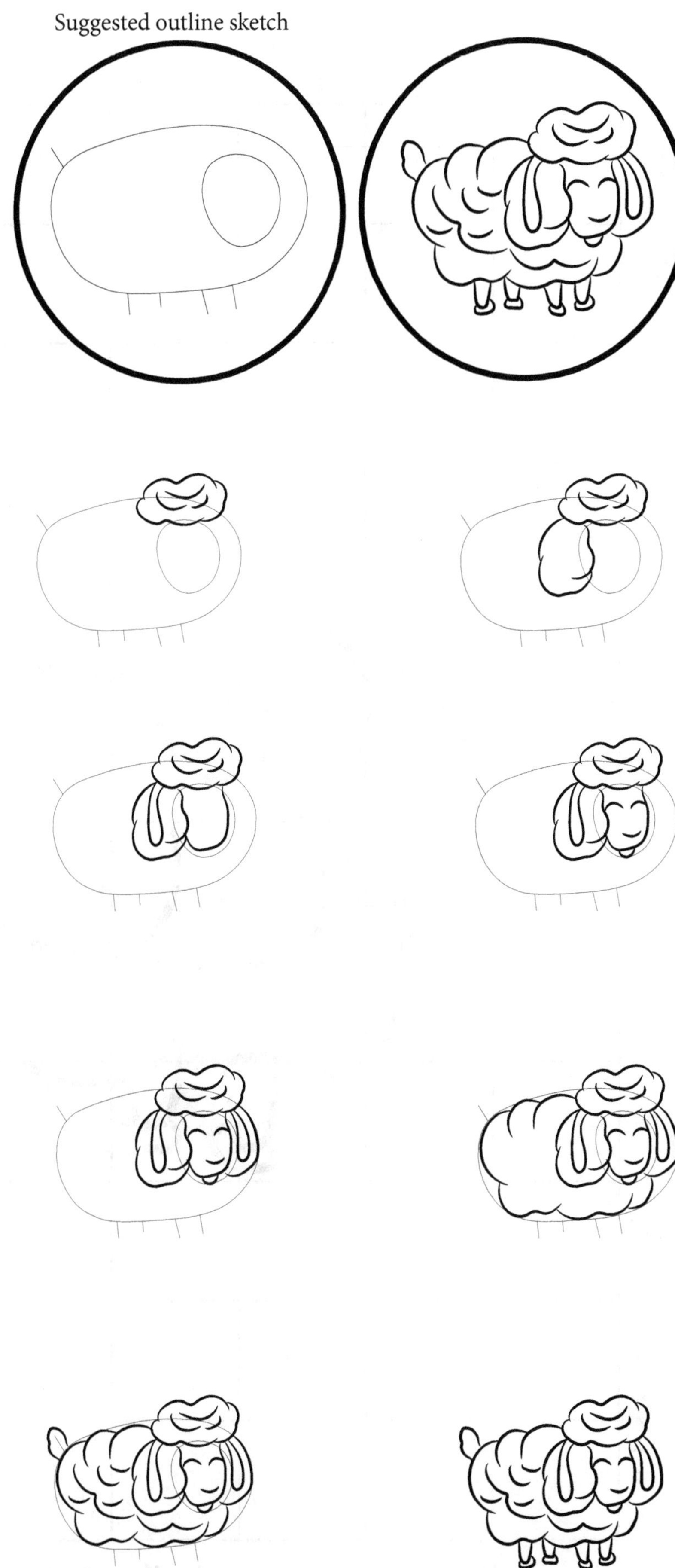

https://www.lipdf.com/product/htdbooks/
Password: 6t5we3

18. Why not experiment with how you hold your pencil? How you hold a pen for handwriting may not be comfortable for drawing.

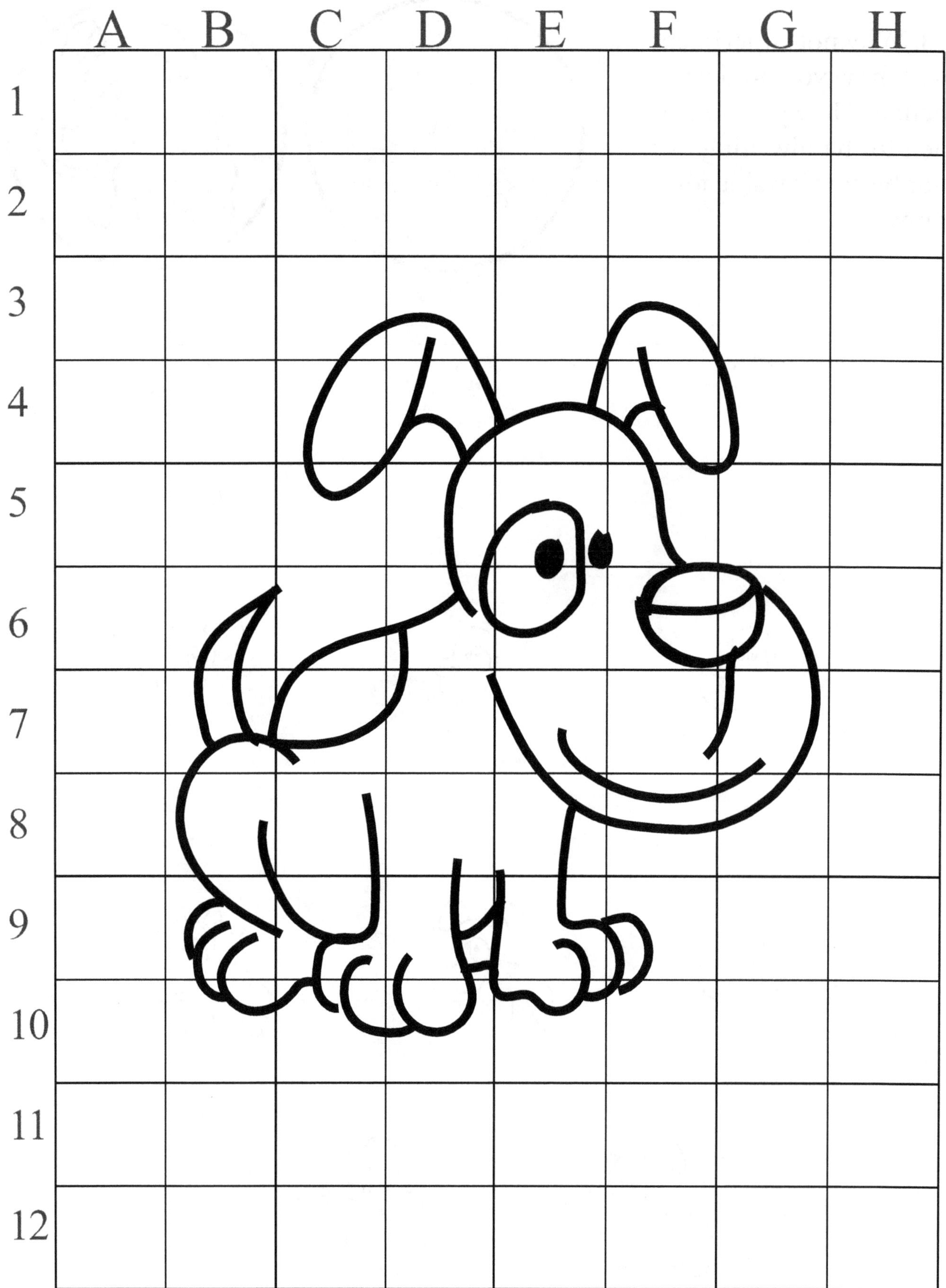

A B C D E F G H
1
2
3
4
5
6
7
8
9
10
11
12

19. Artists never stop learning, so never doubt your talent.

Suggested outline sketch

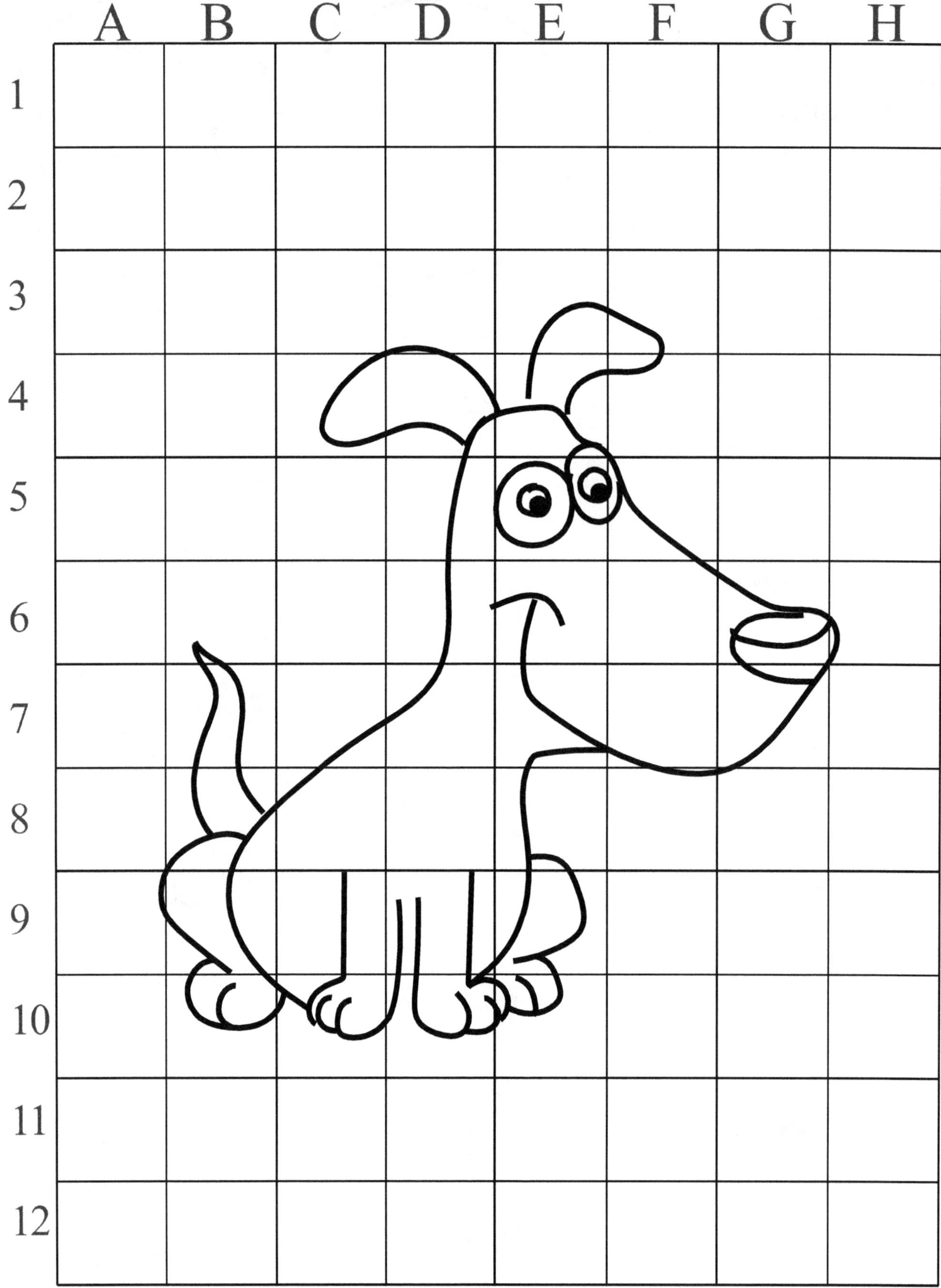

20. There are no rules with art. Feel free to interpret the drawing in your own style.

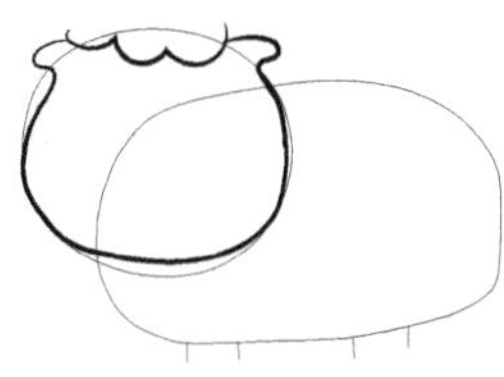

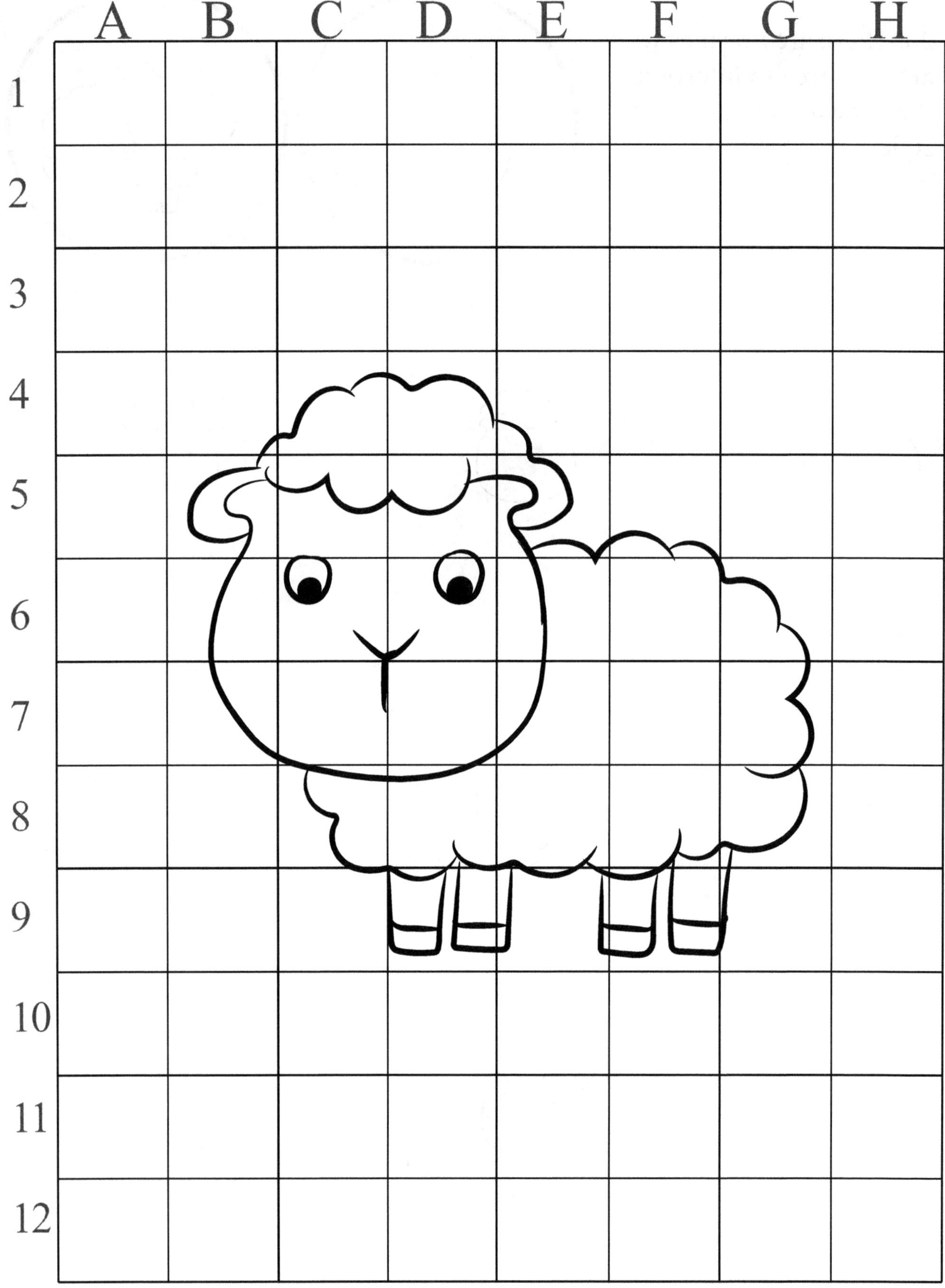

A B C D E F G H
1
2
3
4
5
6
7
8
9
10
11
12

21. Patience is key. If you are getting irritated with your work, leave it for now and come back to it later.

Suggested outline sketch

22. You could have a go at very roughly sketching out the shapes, then going over the lines in pen. Once finished, erase out the rough lines.

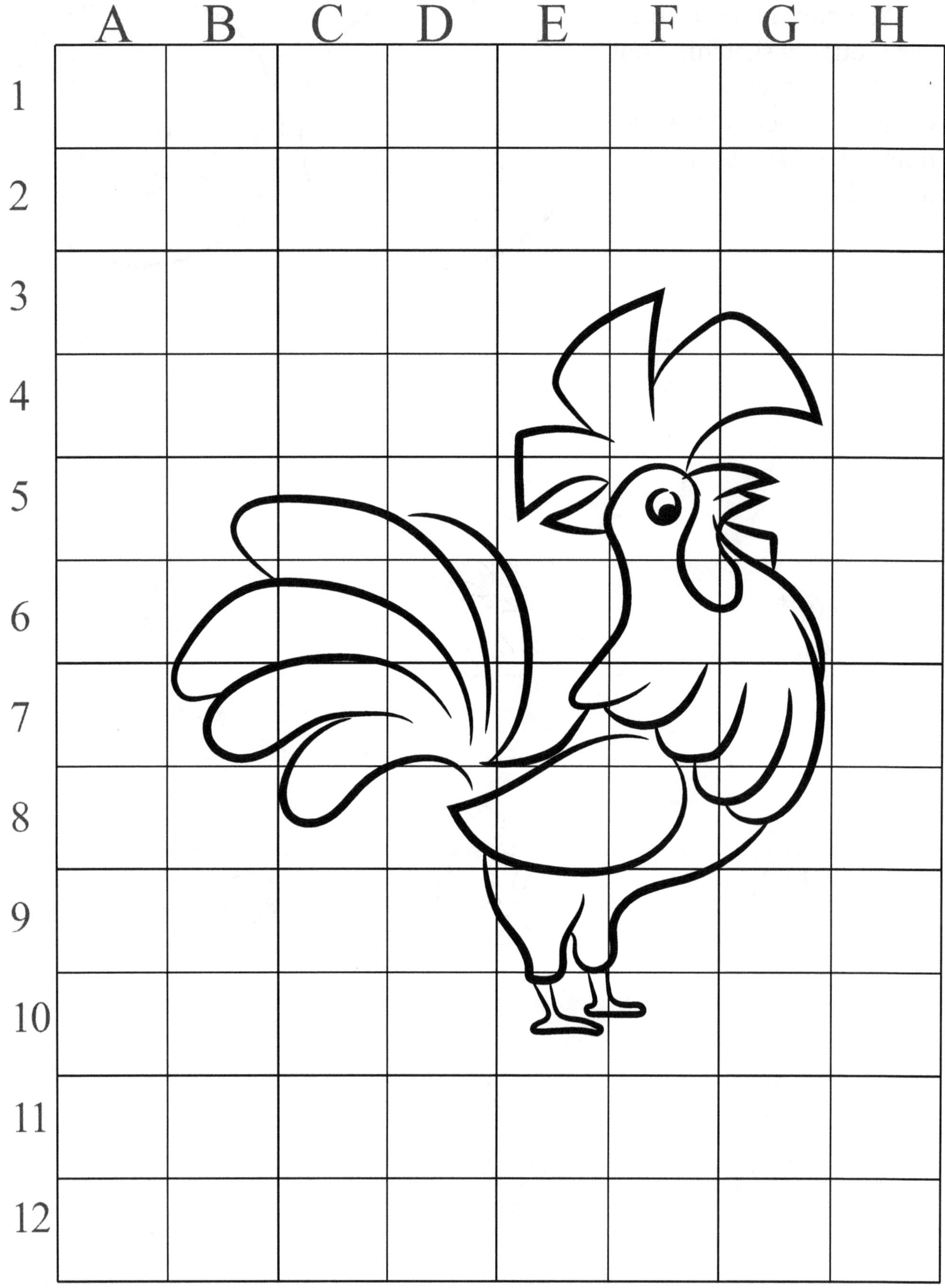

A B C D E F G H
1
2
3
4
5
6
7
8
9
10
11
12

23. Improvement is all about recognising your mistakes, and trying not to make them a second time.

Suggested outline sketch

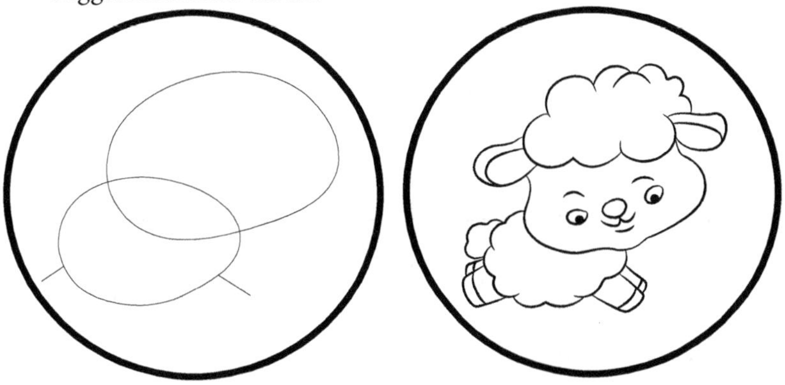

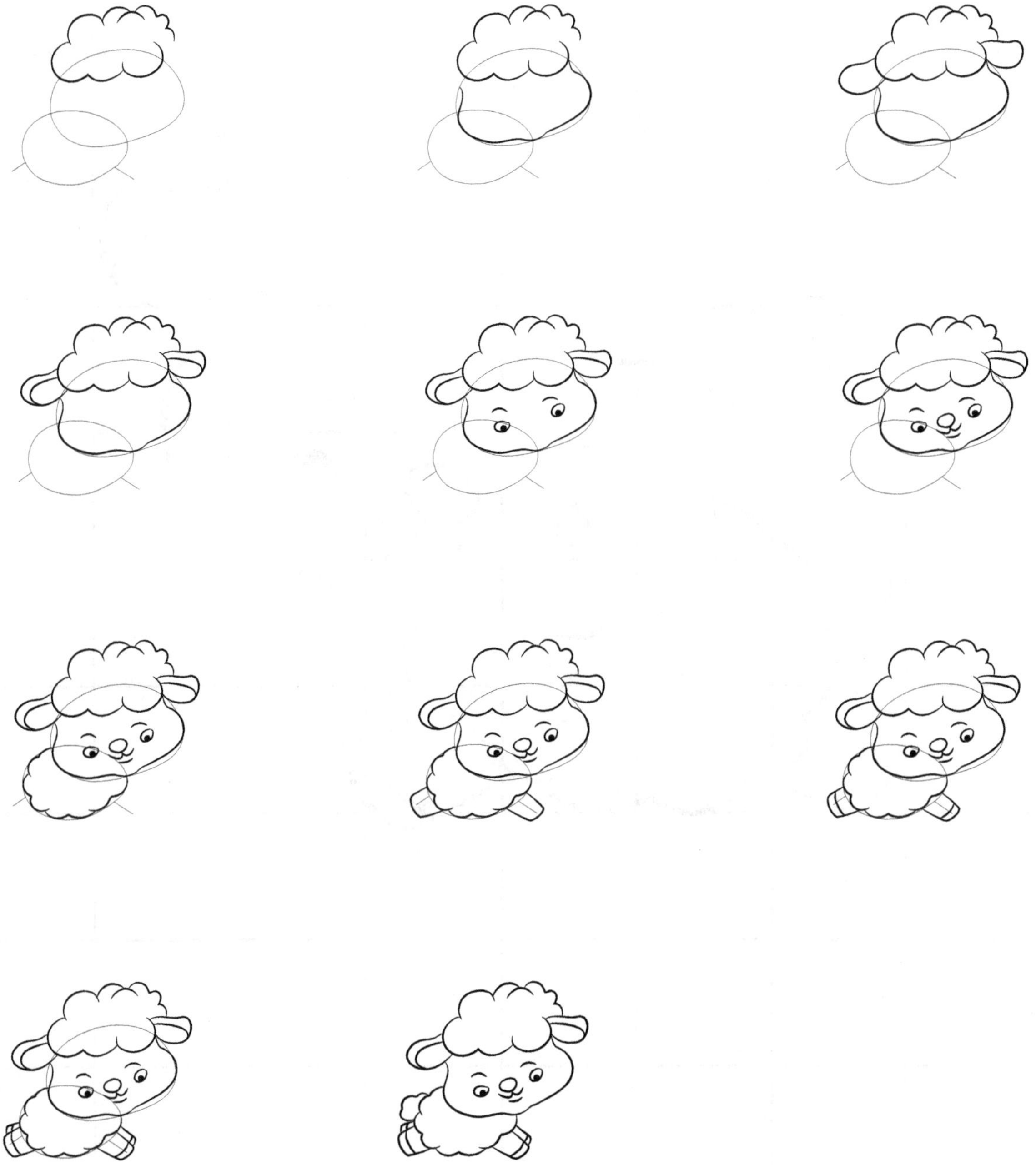

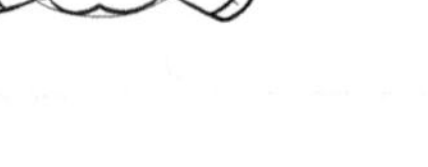

24. Drawing is all trial and error. How do you know how good or bad something looks without even trying to draw it?

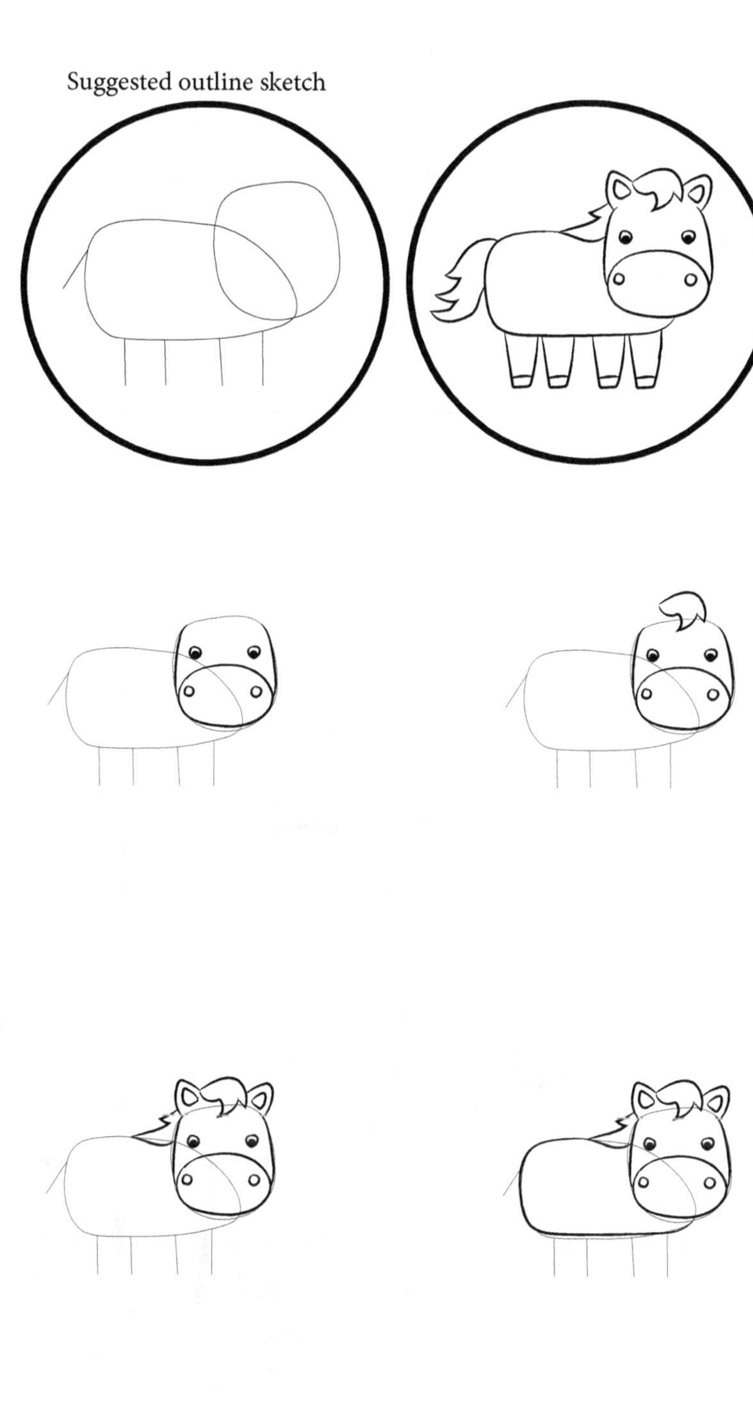
Suggested outline sketch

A B C D E F G H
1
2
3
4
5
6
7
8
9
10
11
12

Suggested outline sketch

27. If you want to, you could practice different types of pencil strokes on a scrap piece of paper. What happens when you press hard with the pencil? What happens when you use the edge of the pencil rather than the point?

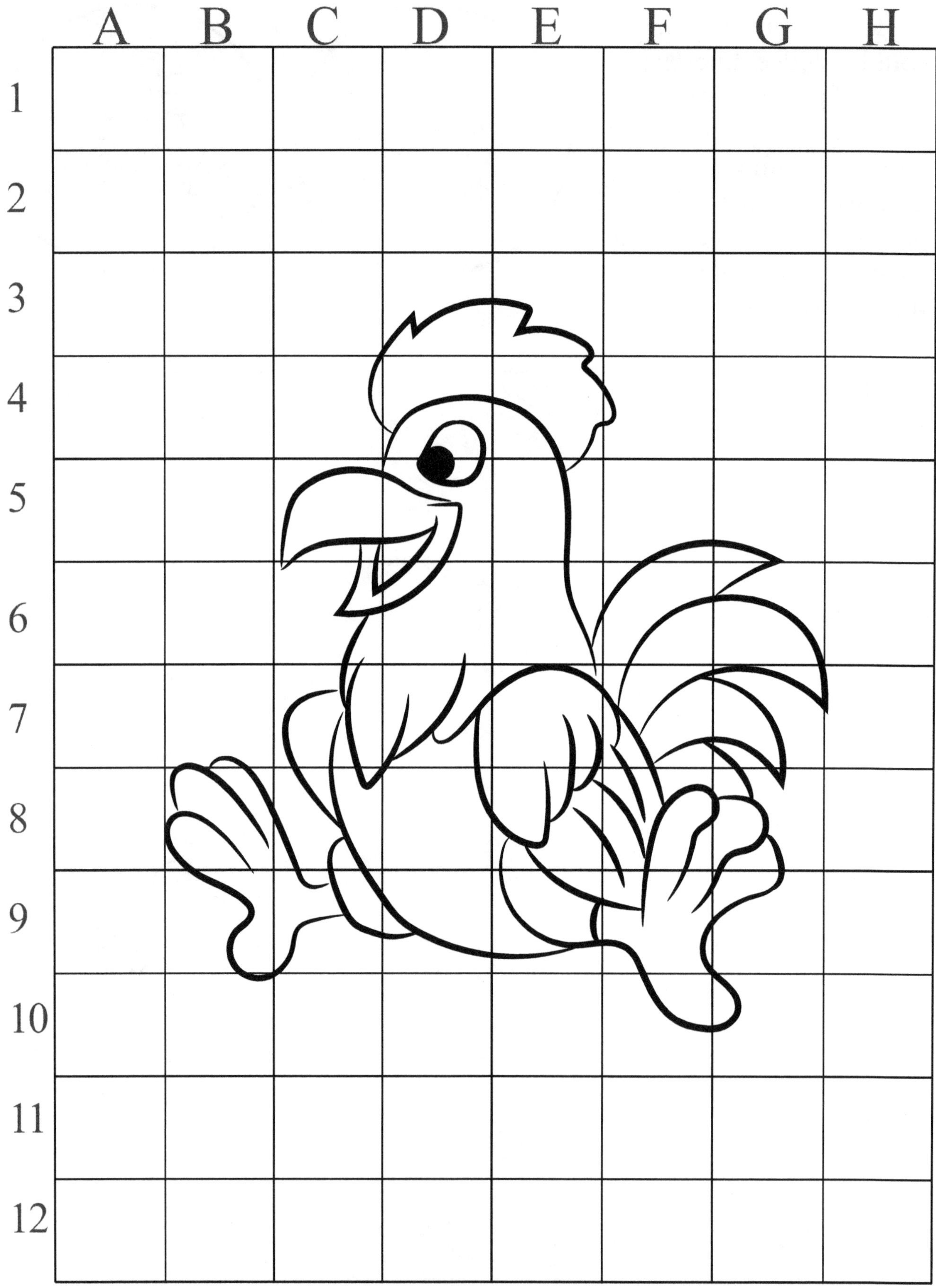

A B C D E F G H
1
2
3
4
5
6
7
8
9
10
11
12

26. Drawing a little everyday will help your drawing improve, stick with it!

Suggested outline sketch

27. Always keep your hand relaxed, you will be surprised to see how your drawing flows on the paper when you aren't pressing too hard with the pencil.

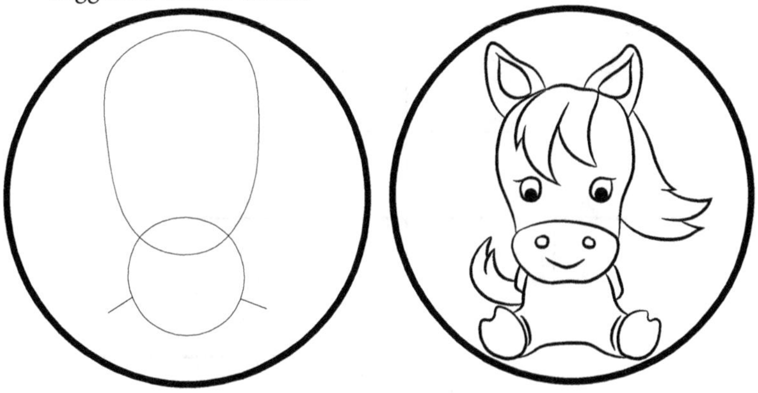

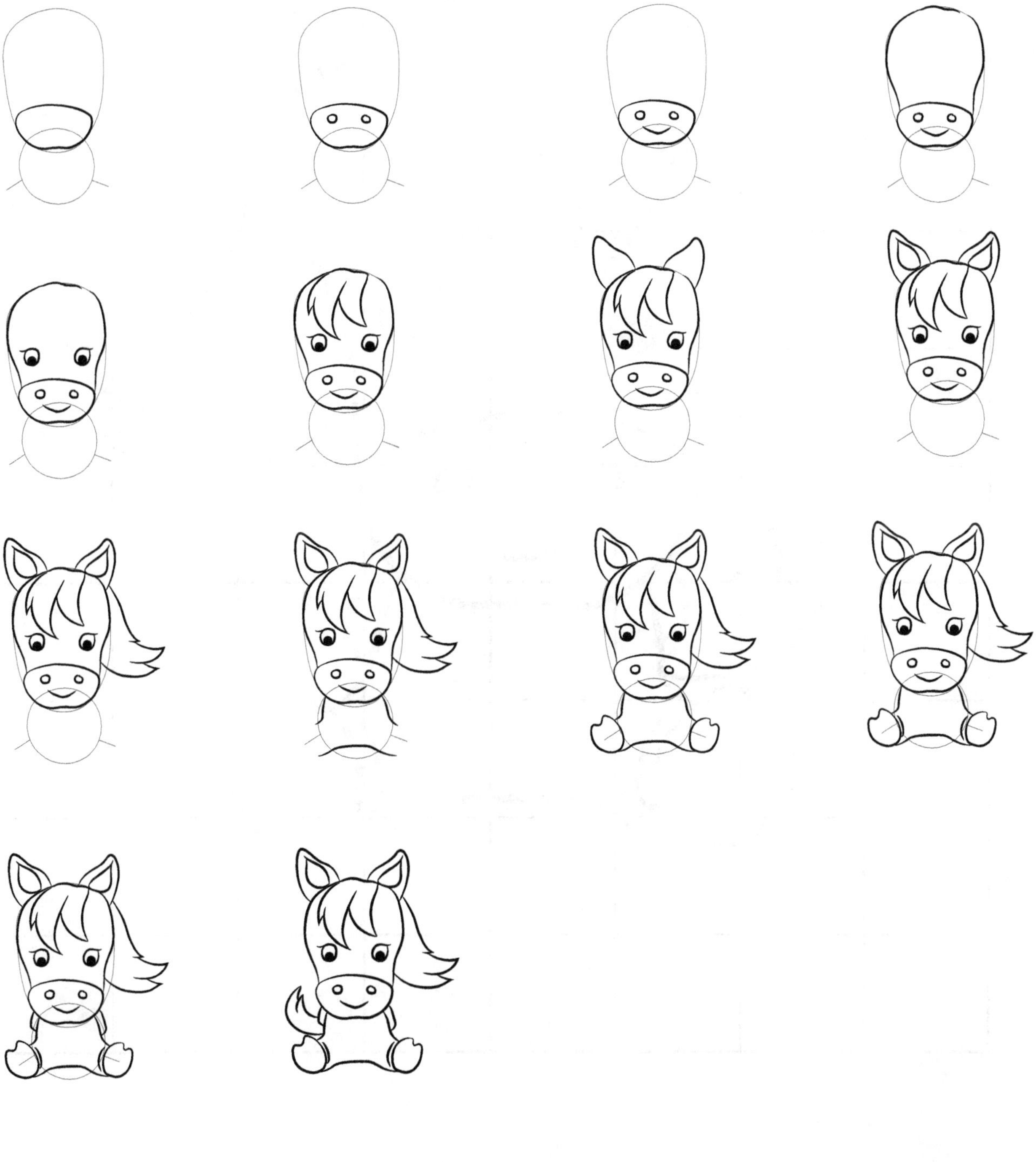

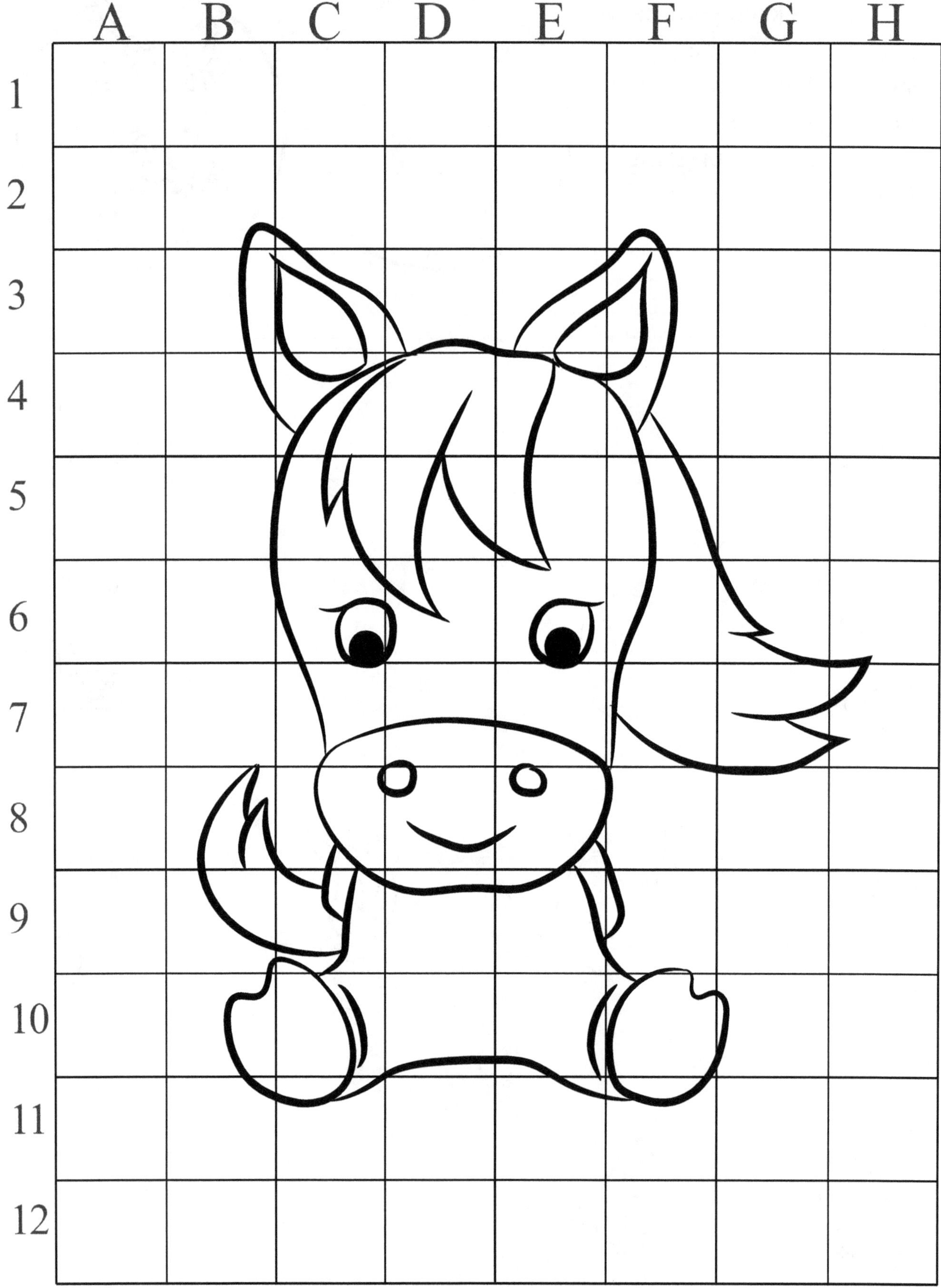
A B C D E F G H
1
2
3
4
5
6
7
8
9
10
11
12

28. Try out a "warm up" exercise before starting your drawing. Have a go at straight, curved and zig zag lines on a scrap piece of paper.

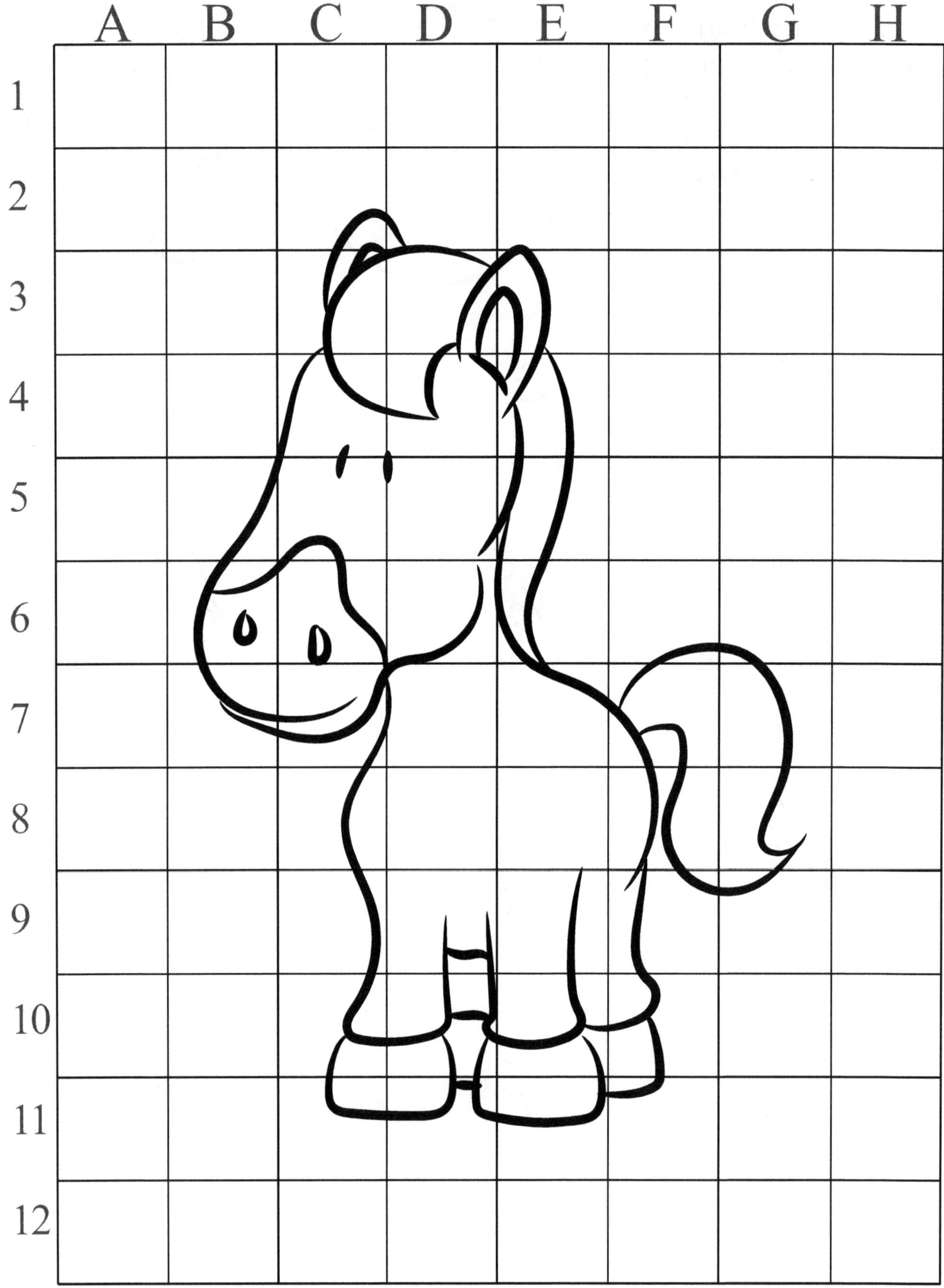

29. If you are struggling to draw a long line, try sketching much shorter lines joined together. You will find your pencil is much easier to control.

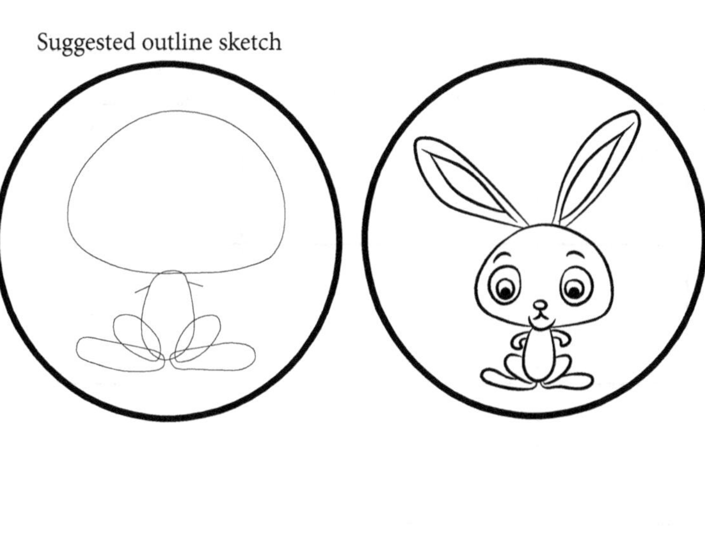

30. If you are struggling to get creative with your drawing, try listening to some music at the same time. As you concentrate on the music, your brain will still be working in the background as you draw.

Suggested outline sketch

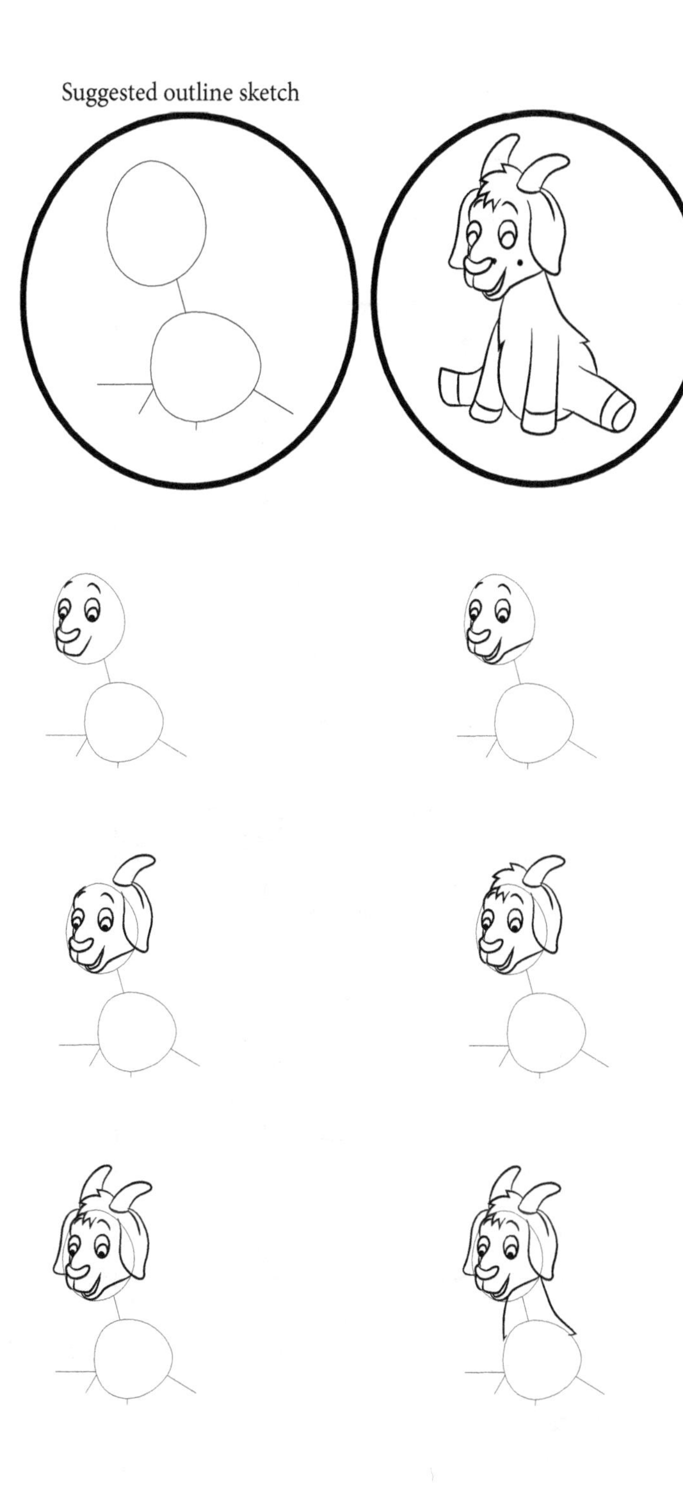

A B C D E F G H
1
2
3
4
5
6
7
8
9
10
11
12

31. Much like handwriting, everyone's drawing technique is unique, so don't feel disheartened if you draw differently to your friends and siblings – they probably feel the same way!

Suggested outline sketch

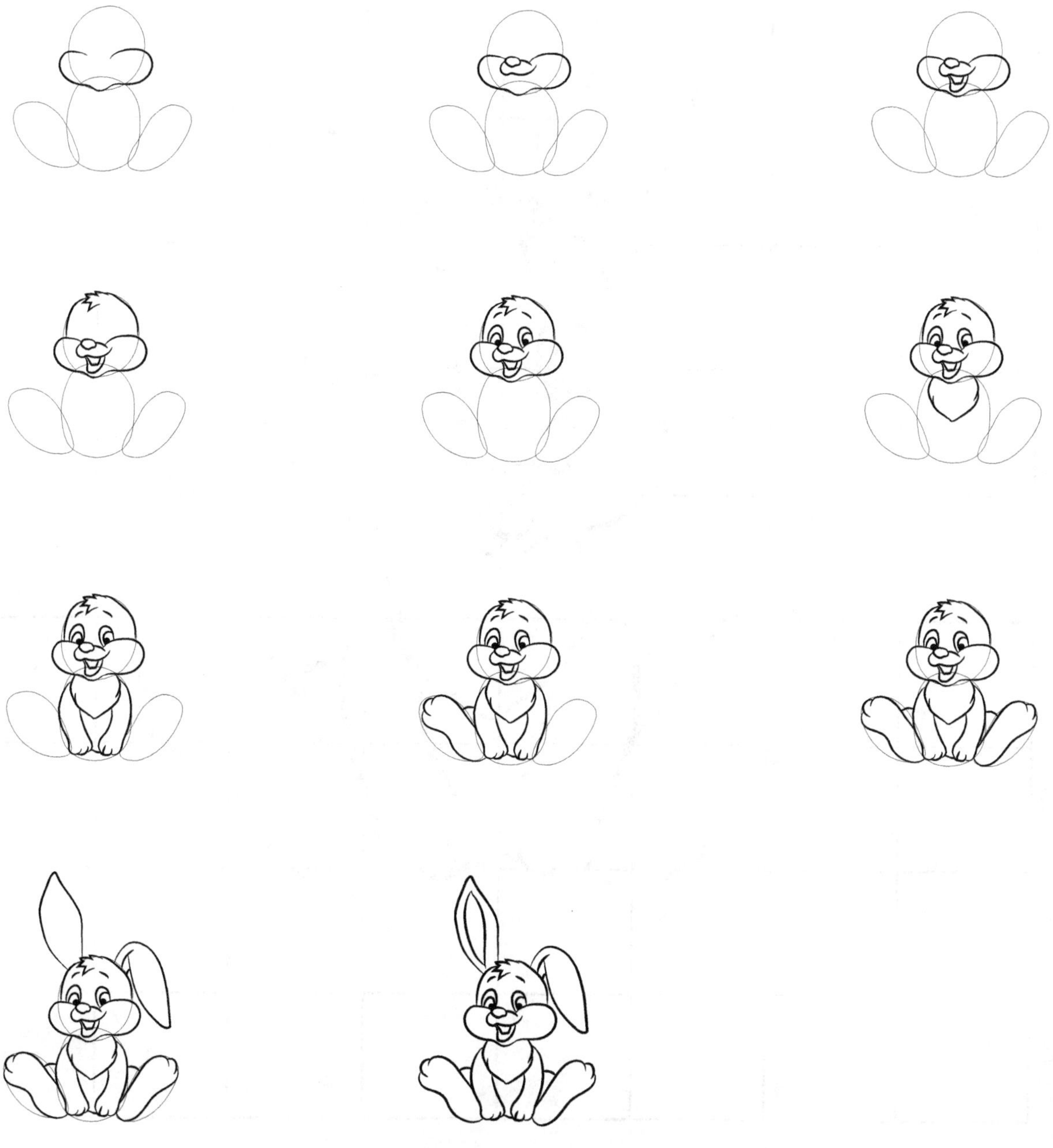

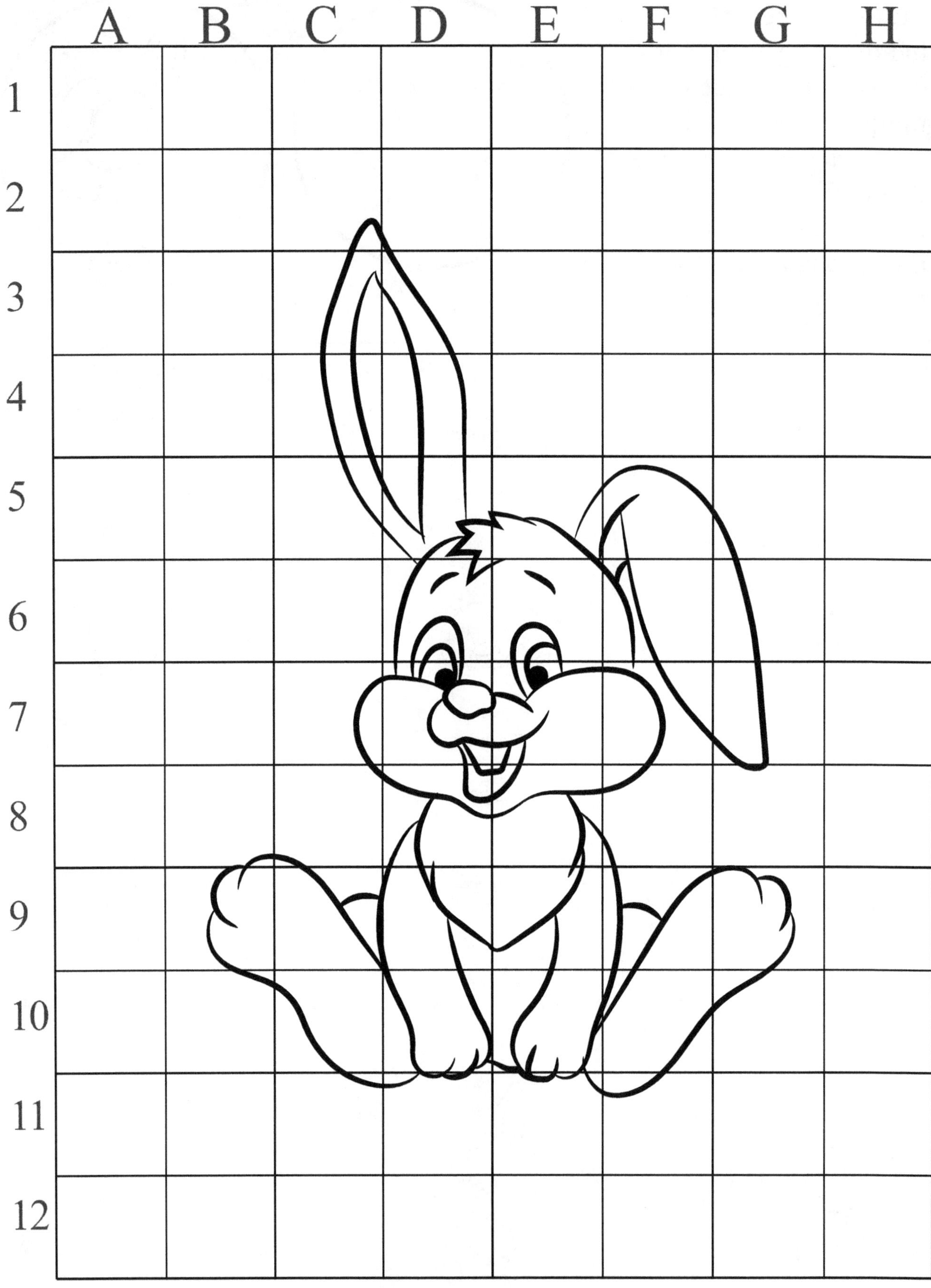

32. Stay creative! You don't
have to copy the image
exactly as I have laid it out,
just use the lines as a guide.

Suggested outline sketch

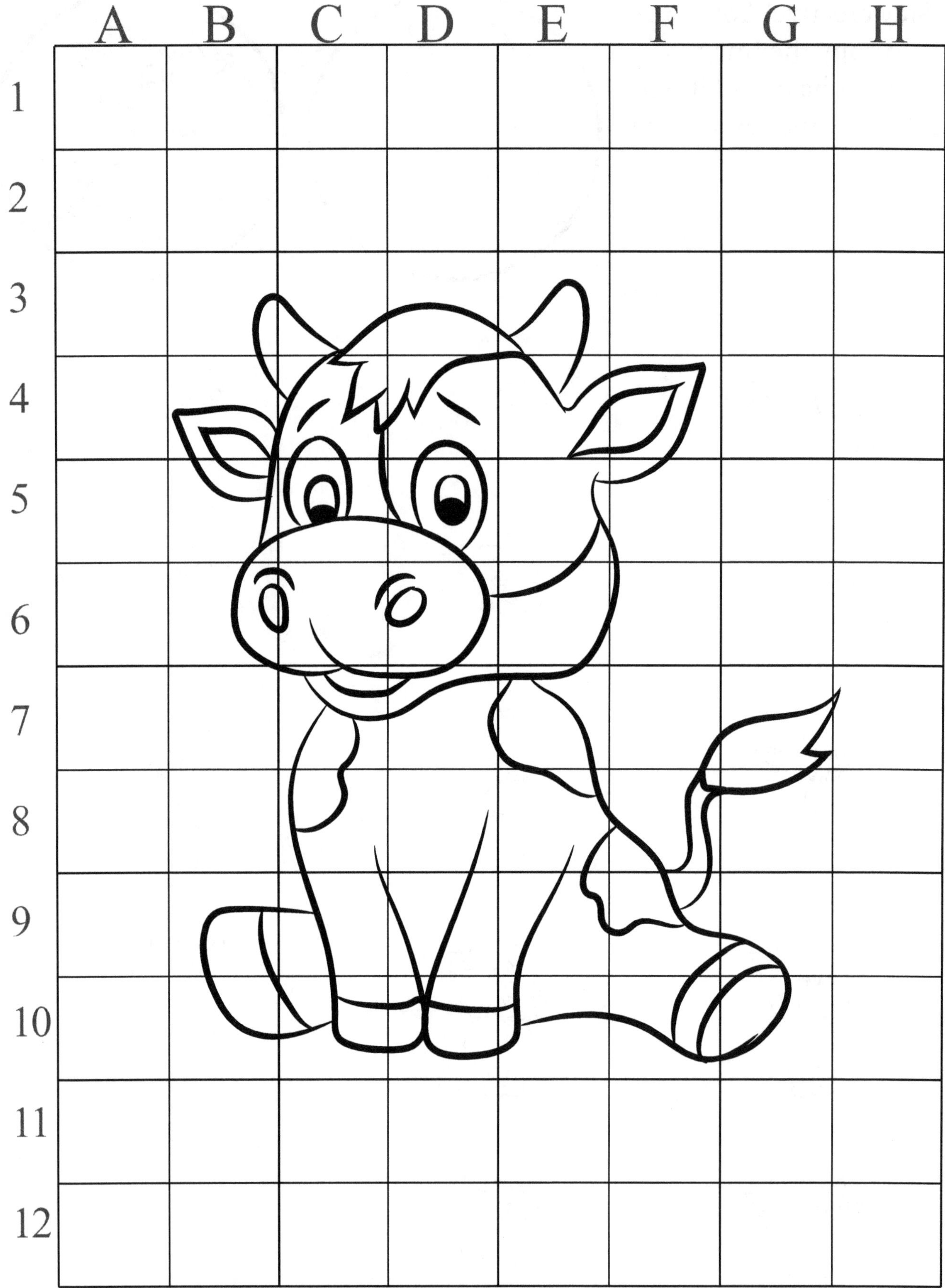

A B C D E F G H
1
2
3
4
5
6
7
8
9
10
11
12

33. Try not to get annoyed
if what you've drawn on
the paper isn't as you had
envisioned, keep on going
and you'll find that every
pencil stroke will
eventually come together.

Suggested outline sketch

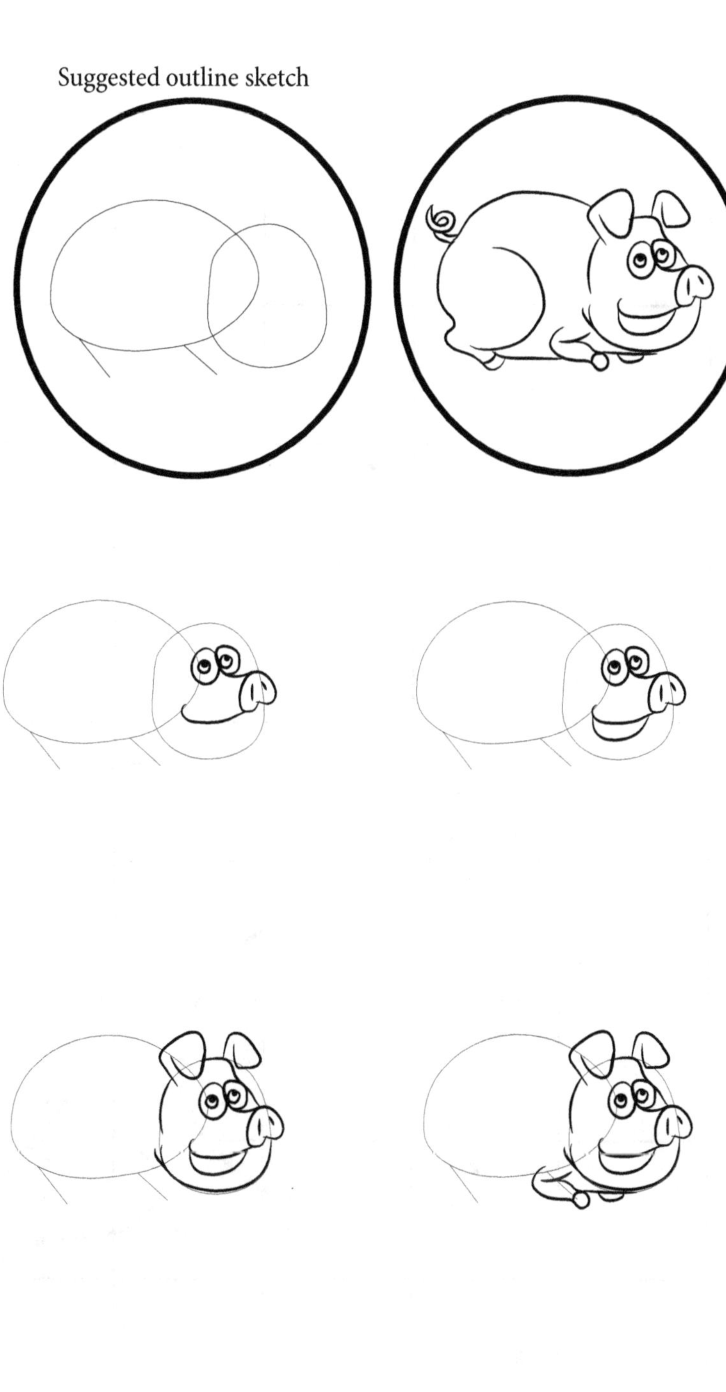

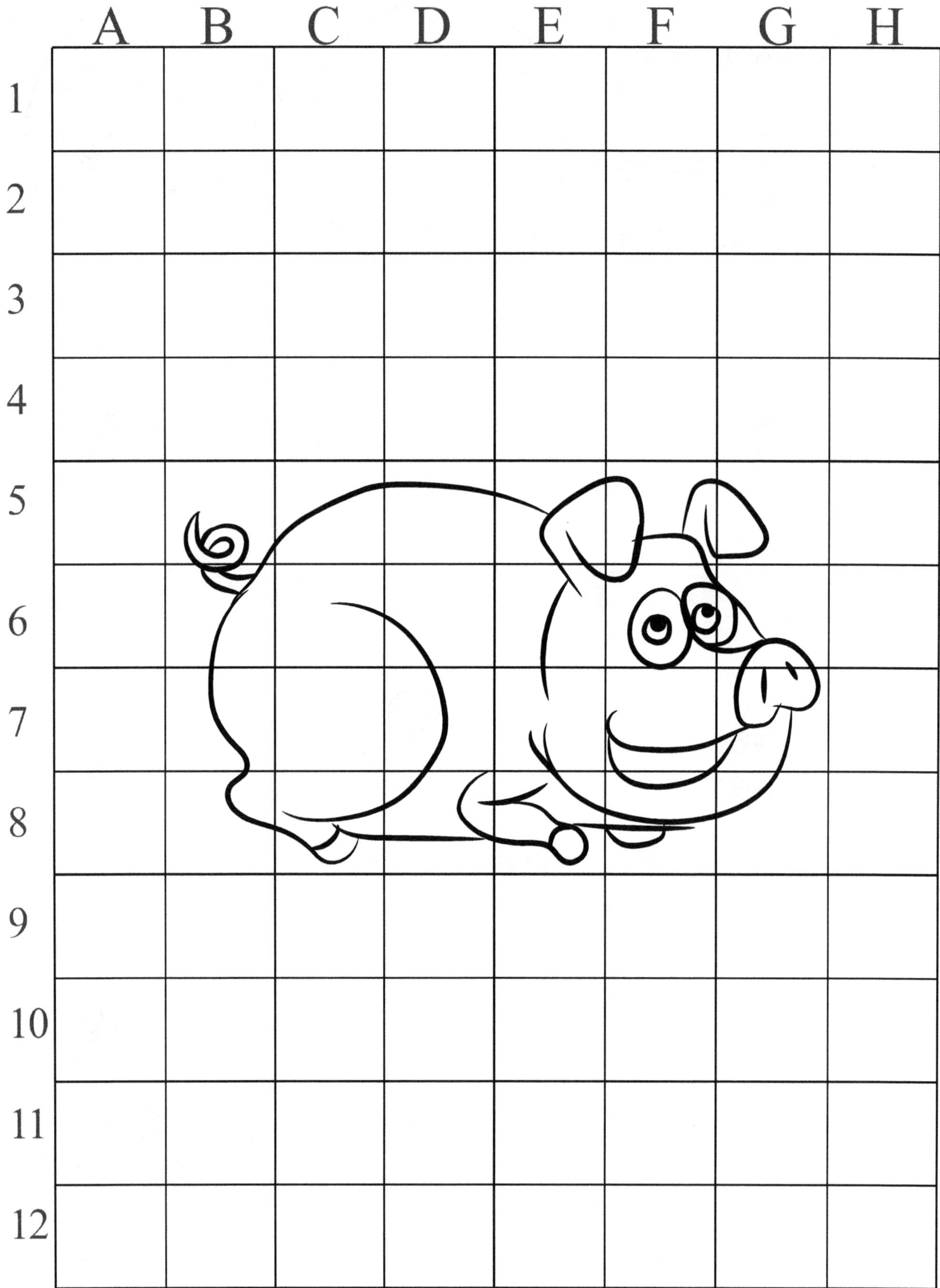

A B C D E F G H
1
2
3
4
5
6
7
8
9
10
11
12

34. If you are becoming frustrated and finding the next step of the drawing a challenge, keep yourself calm and go back a few steps. By repeating the last few steps you may find this helps you flow into the step you are finding difficult.

Suggested outline sketch

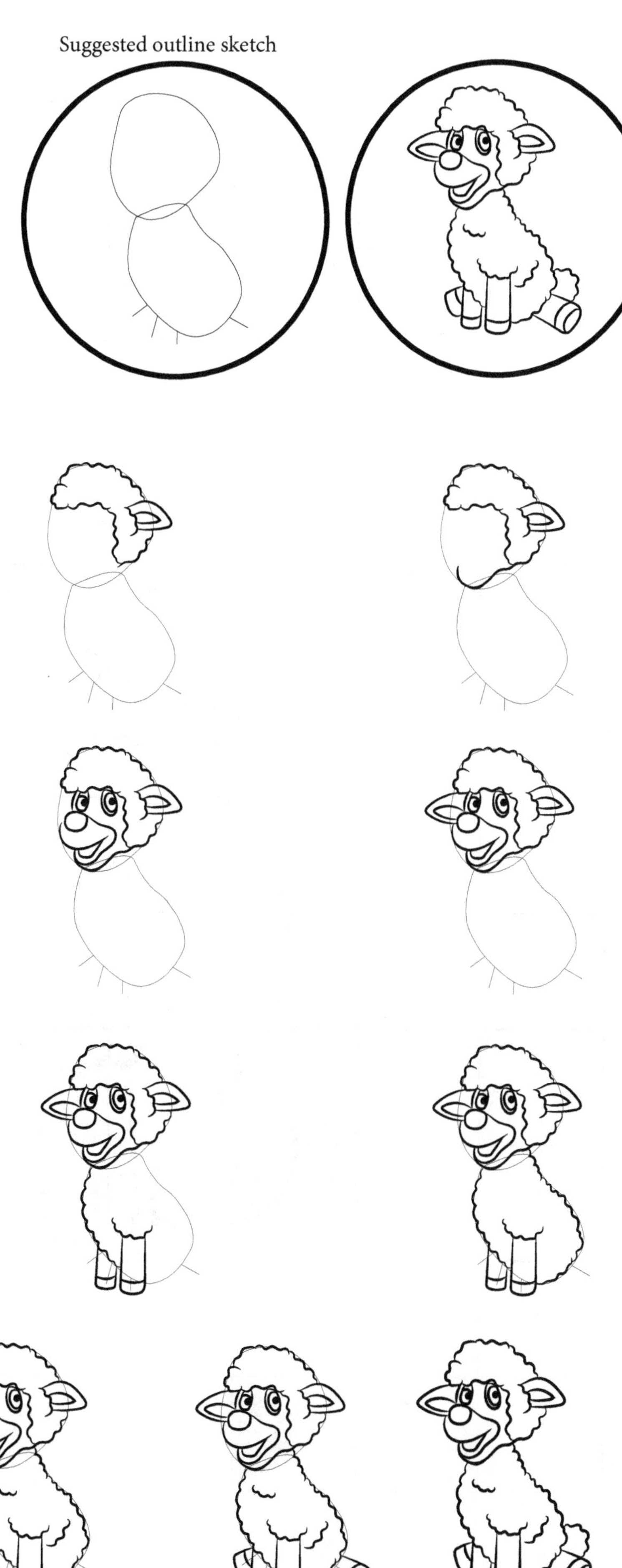

A B C D E F G H
1
2
3
4
5
6
7
8
9
10
11
12

35. Everybody will make a mistake following this book, but perhaps that 'mistake' could actually become part of the drawing itself!

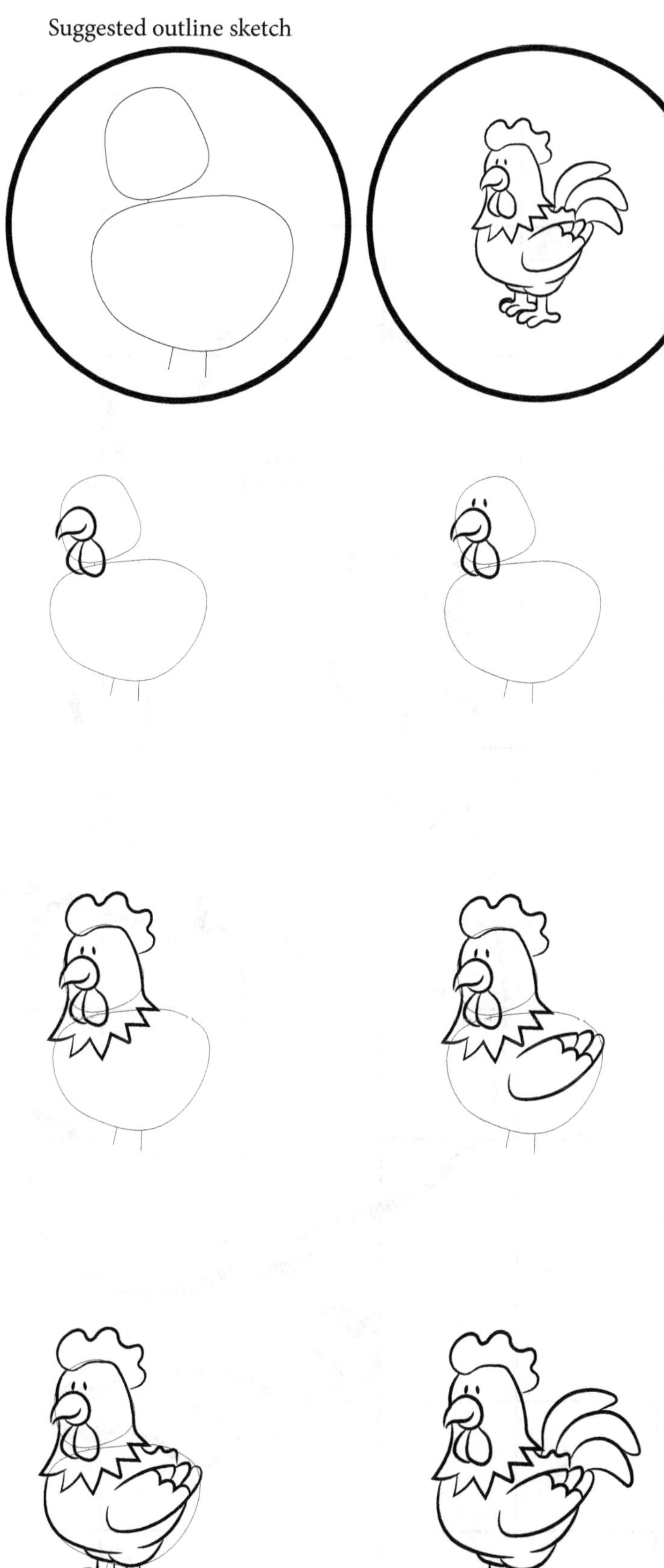

36. Art is all about interpretation and expression, so use the images as a guide and alter them to your own preferences.

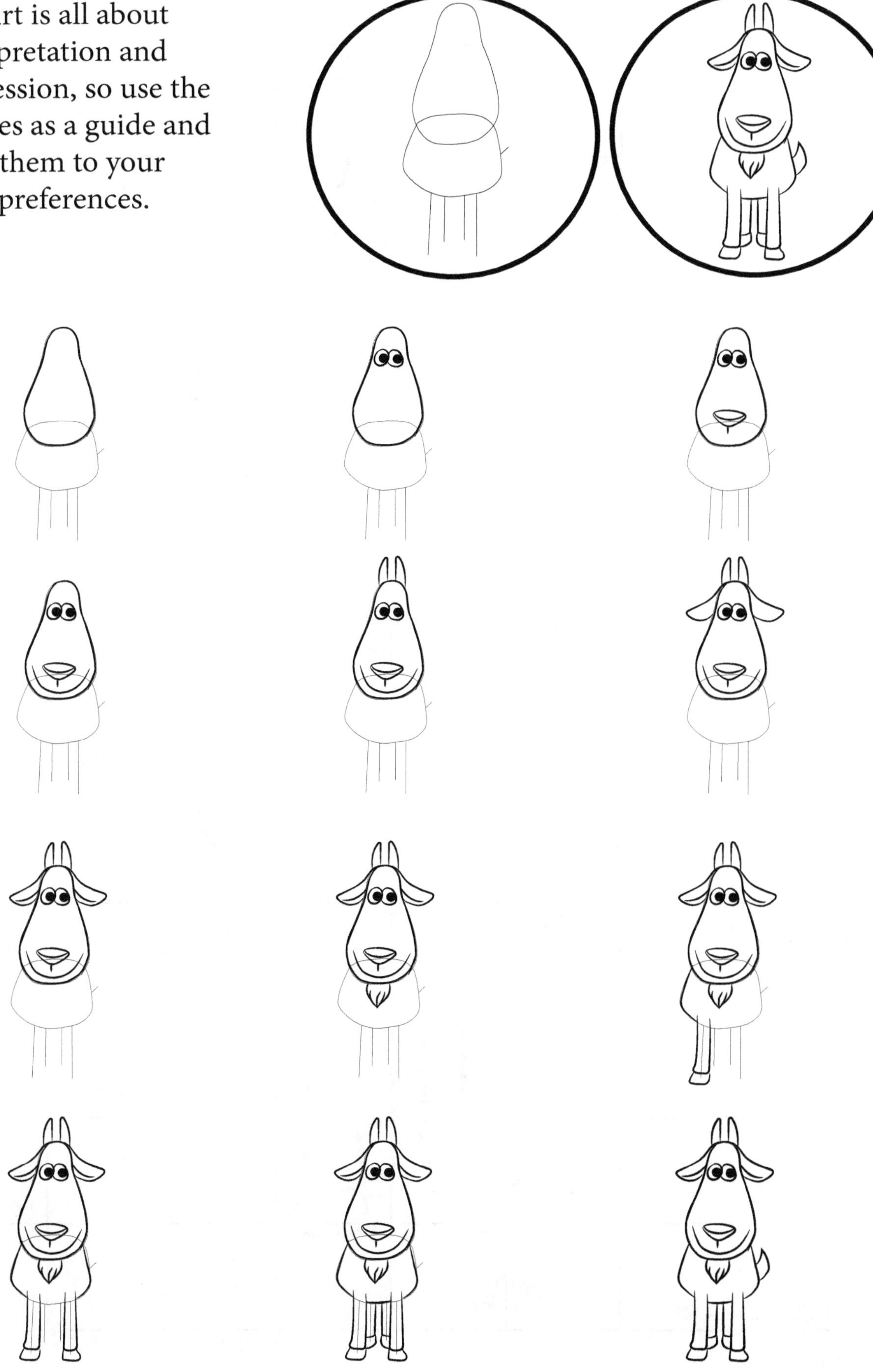

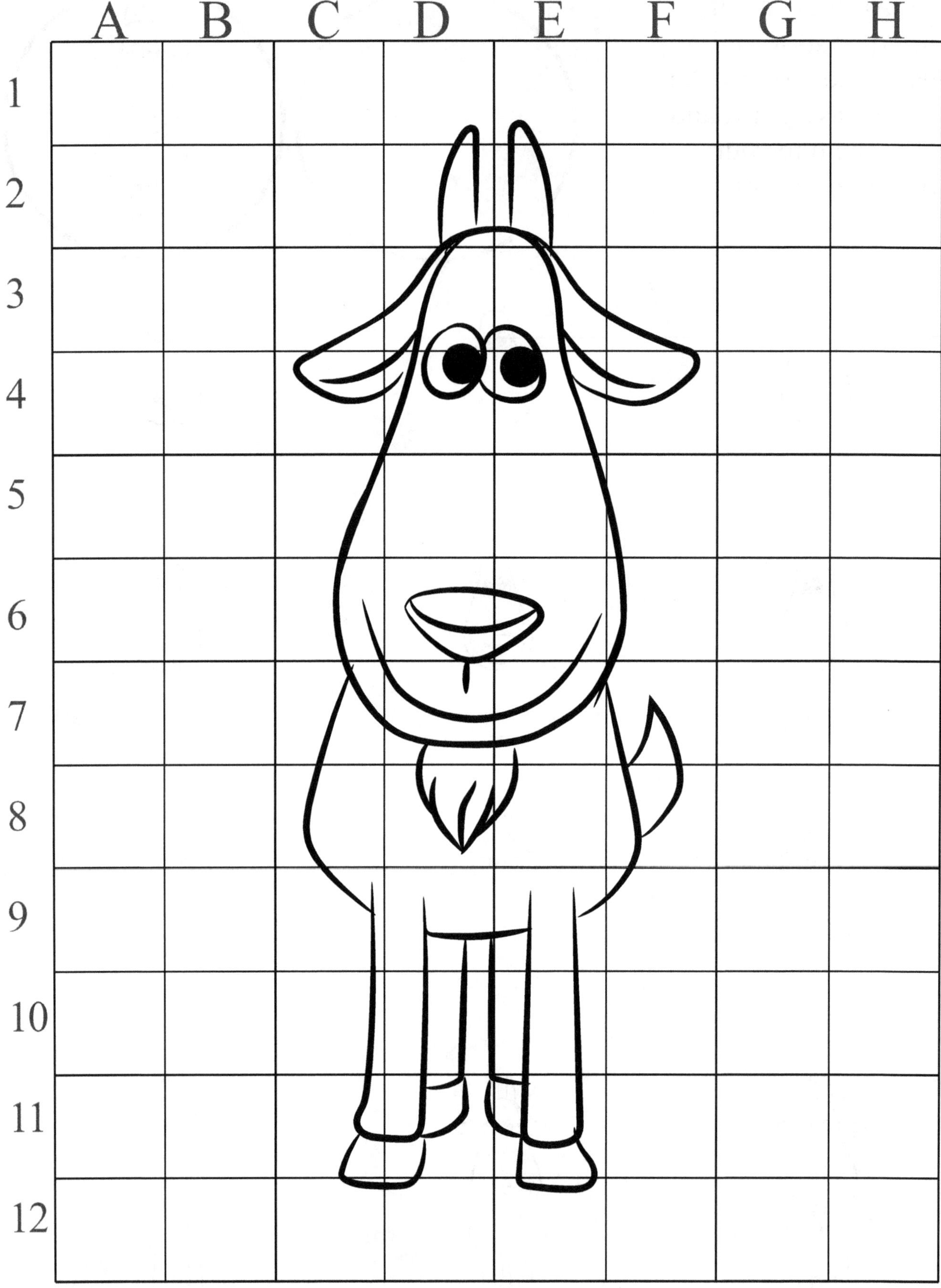

37. If you keep up with drawing every day, you will be surprised at the improvements you'll see in your sketches!

Suggested outline sketch

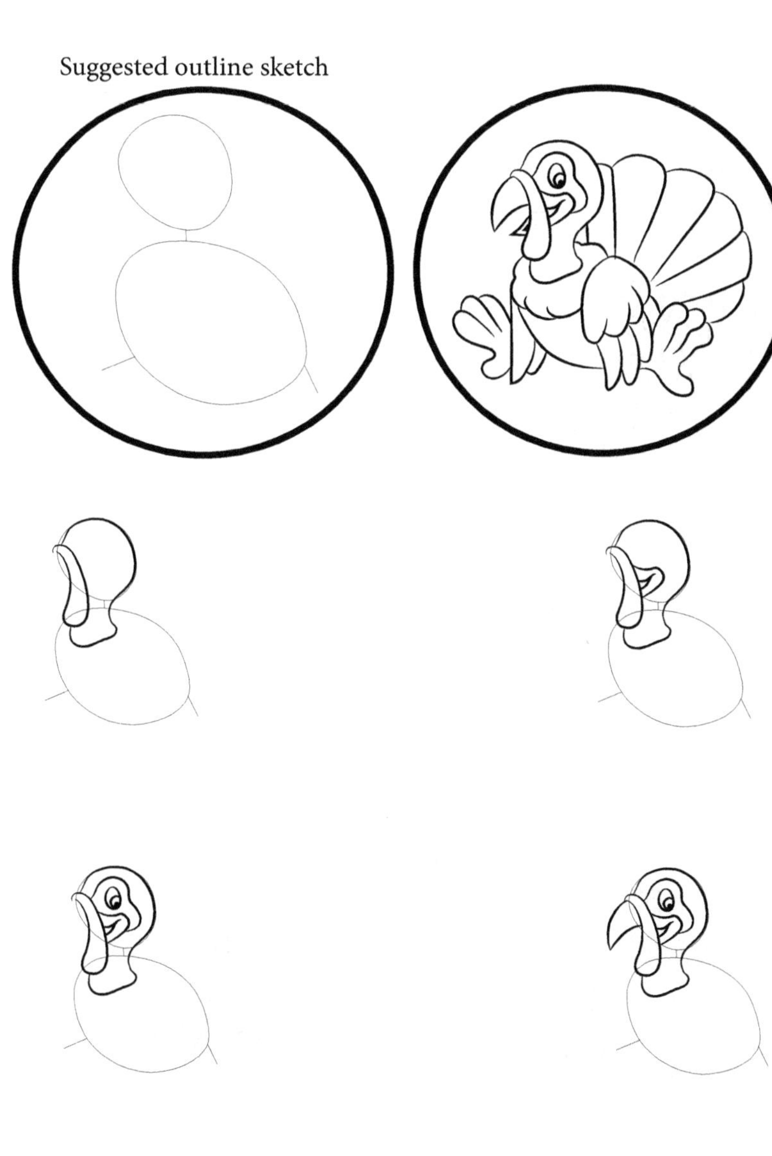

38. Have a go at using
ellipses (circles that have
an irregular shape) to plan
out your sketch, then
gradually build the image
from there.

Suggested outline sketch

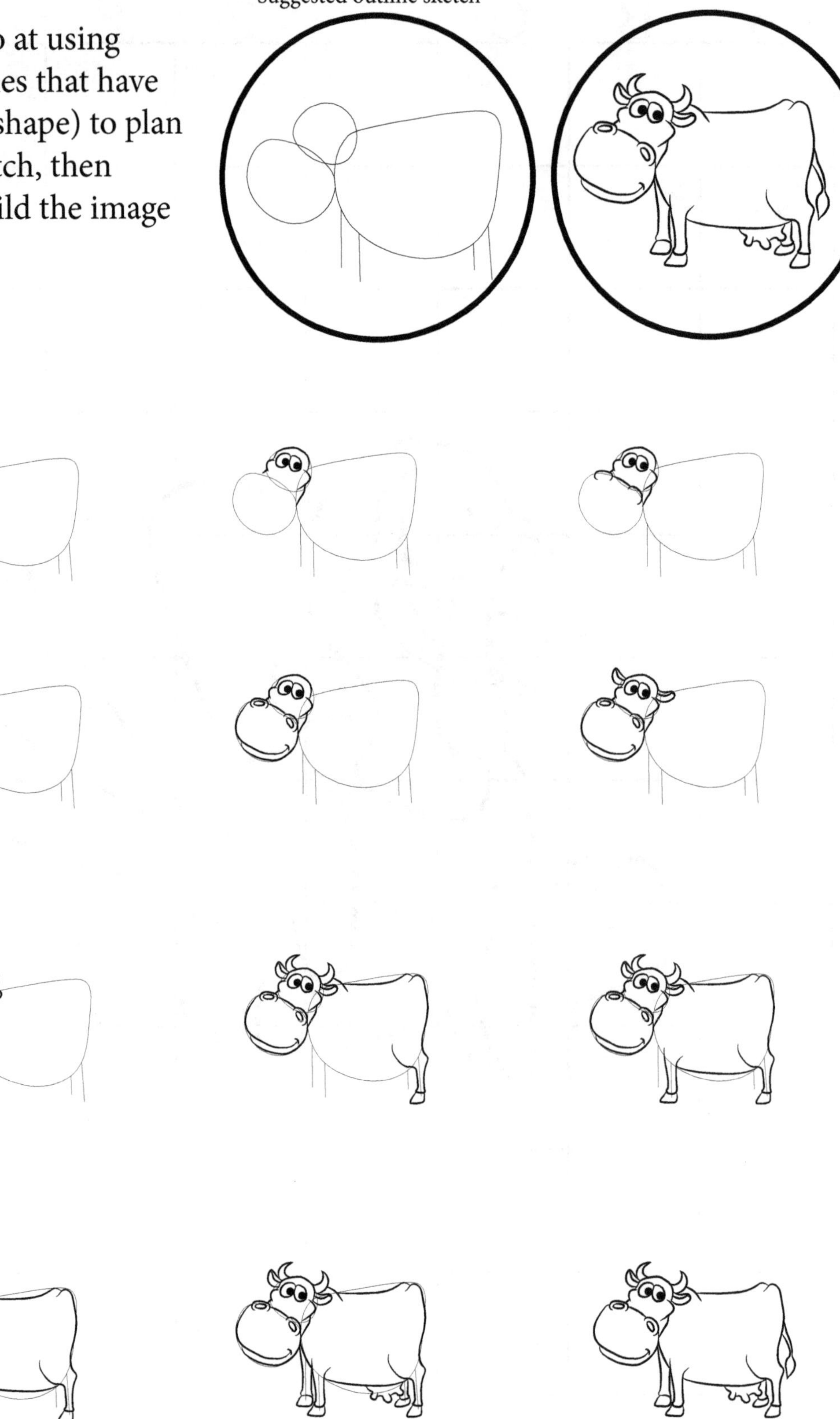

39. Draw a basic sketch with rough outlines of the head and the body. This sketch is approximate and does not need to be exact.

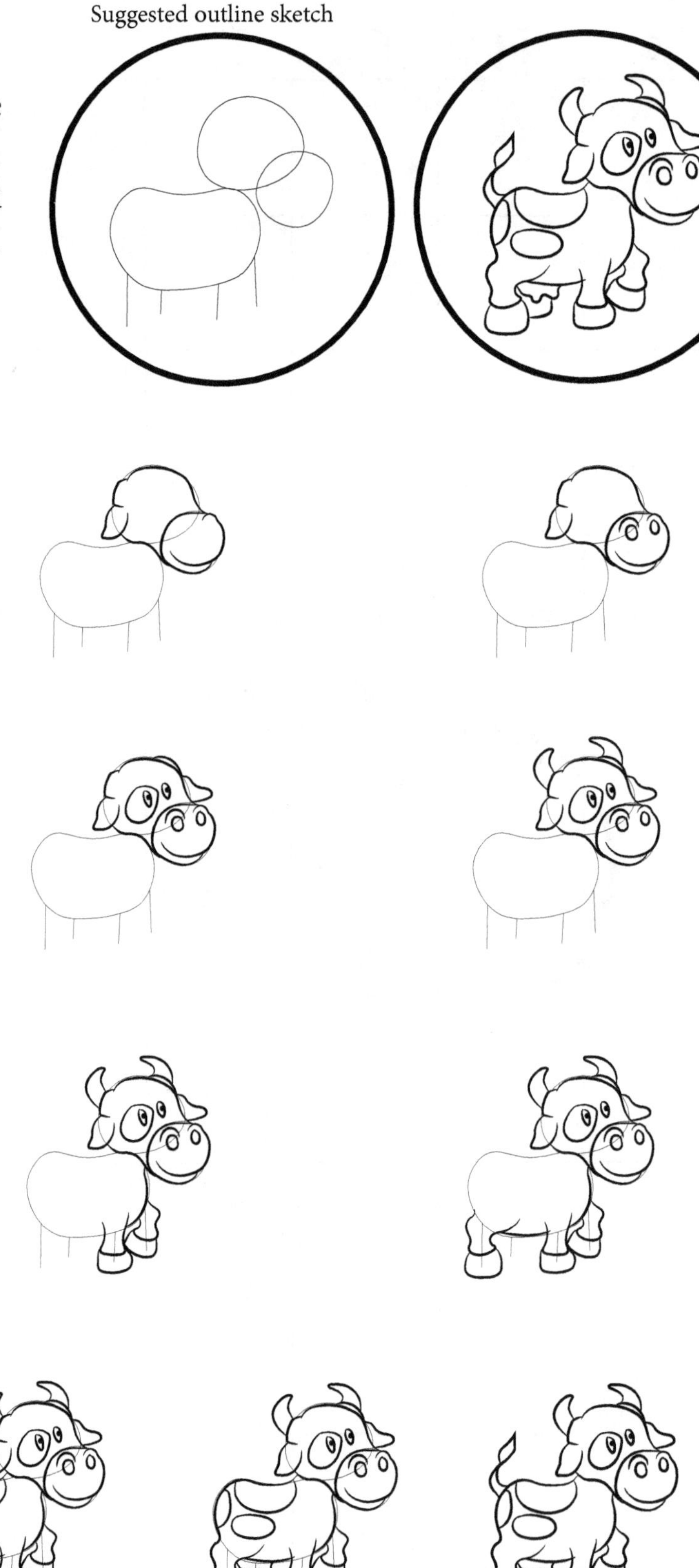

40. Creativity does not necessarily involve logic. The brain is very good as solving pattern challenges if you give it a chance.

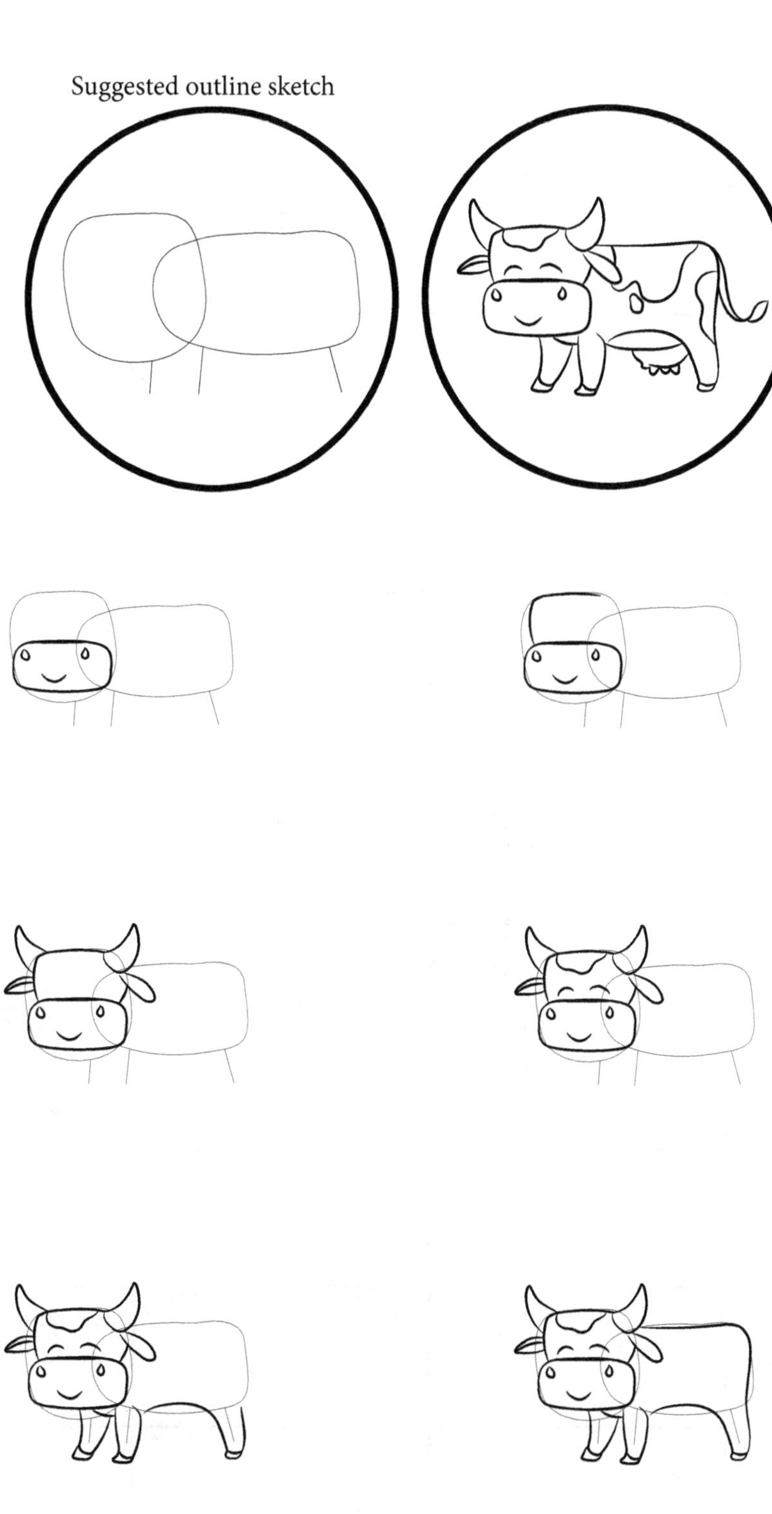

A B C D E F G H
1
2
3
4
5
6
7
8
9
10
11
12

CPSIA information can be obtained
at www.ICGtesting.com
Printed in the USA
BVHW011451180921
617010BV00043B/191